"Having worked around the globe with families experiencing disability, I have unfortunately seen firsthand that fathers of children with disabilities are typically absent, ashamed, or apathetic. But I have seen others. I have watched fathers live a different story and lead their entire family—including their loved one with a disability—into a deeper, more meaningful life. Jeff and Becky remind us that these men don't just happen. They are the ones who lean in where others flee."

—**MATTHEW MOONEY**, cofounder of 99 Balloons, author of *A Story Unfinished*, and host of *The Atypical Podcast*

"Finally, a book written specifically for fathers of kids with special needs and disabilities. *Common Man, Extraordinary Call* speaks directly to dads in their language because the author, the late Jeff Davidson, is their brother. Davidson speaks frankly about how he failed his wife, Becky, and son after Jon Alex was diagnosed with multiple special needs. Jeff describes his remarkable transformation from absent dad to loving father as he came to comprehend the gift he and his wife had been given in Jon Alex. With love and eloquence, Davidson encourages dads to join him in the fight to protect, parent, and provide for their children.

"Becky Davidson, who completed the book after Jeff died unexpectedly, describes the powerful legacy her husband left for her, their son, and the community of special-needs dads. Becky reveals to readers what those blessed to meet her husband know to be true. What God did for Jeff, this humble father vows, God will do for the ordinary men who accept his call to become the extraordinary leaders of their special-needs families."

—**JOLENE PHILO**, author of the Different Dream Parenting Series and *Does My Child Have PTSD?*

"When we got our son's autism diagnosis in 2010, we each reacted differently to the news. The testimony of another special-needs dad was what God used to get us on the same page and moving forward together. That's why we believe Jeff's message specifically for men is so important. Jeff has a pastor's heart for coming alongside dads in the toughest season of their lives. And his words will equip men to engage in the battle, encourage their families, and build endurance for the path ahead. Jeff lived out the message of this book, and we are so thankful Becky was able to complete this mission."

—**DR. LEE PEOPLES**, pastor of Heights Baptist Church, Alvin, Texas, and **SANDRA PEOPLES**, author of *Unexpected Blessings*

"Jeff Davidson was a true champion of fathers of kids with special needs. His ability to speak into the lives of men struggling with the feelings of hopelessness and loss common to dads in families impacted by disability is irreplaceable. *Common Man, Extraordinary Call* tangibly demonstrates God's love for special-needs dads through Jeff's words of wisdom and encouragement to men who missed out on the blessing of knowing him in this life."

—**STEPHEN GRCEVICH**, MD, president and founder of Key Ministry, and author of *Mental Health and the Church*

COMMON MAN, EXTRAORDINARY CALL

Thriving as the Dad of a Child with Special Needs

JEFF DAVIDSON with BECKY DAVIDSON

Common Man, Extraordinary Call: Thriving as the Dad of a Child with Special Needs

Published by Kregel Publications, a division of Kregel Inc., 2450 Oak Industrial Dr. NE, Grand Rapids, MI 49505.

The authors and publisher are not engaged in rendering medical or psychological services, and this book is not intended as a guide to diagnose or treat medical or psychological problems. If medical, psychological, or other expert assistance is required, the reader should seek the services of a health-care provider or certified counselor.

The persons and events portrayed in this book have been used with permission.

Published in association with the literary agency of Credo Communications, LLC, Grand Rapids, Michigan, www.CredoCommunications.net.

ISBN 978-0-8254-4545-3, print
ISBN 978-0-8254-7519-1, epub

Printed in the United States of America
19 20 21 22 23 24 25 26 27 28 / 5 4 3 2 1

To my father,
Bill Davidson,
who taught me everything I know
about how to be a dad.

"The Lord gets his best soldiers out of
the highlands of affliction."

CHARLES SPURGEON

CONTENTS

FOREWORD

The Bravest Man I Ever Knew

A Tribute from Retired Master Sergeant Rick Imel

The bravest man I ever knew never served in the military. That is quite a statement because I served my country for twenty-three years and have witnessed bravery on the battlefield in spades. The bravest man I ever knew had a deep love and respect for men and women in the armed forces. He would buy meals for those in uniform anonymously. He would place signs in his yard thanking vets on Veterans Day and Memorial Day. He studied military leaders to gain insight on leadership. He would listen with rapt attention whenever I let my guard down and discussed my military experiences, but he never heard angry shots fired, never dragged a wounded comrade off the battlefield, never applied a field dressing to a wounded soldier's jaw ripped apart by shrapnel, and never had to calm his men and steel them for the fight that was to come.

The bravest man I ever knew was my friend Jeff Davidson. He fought an unseen Enemy. He would often tell me how much he respected me for my service, yet he was too humble to realize that his bravery was much greater than anything I had ever done on the battlefield. My enemy was simply those who were trying to kill me or my men, and we were trained and had the means to strike back.

Jeff's Enemy was unseen. He could not fire back. He had to maintain his faith in God and God's plan for his life.

Jeff gave up a lucrative career because God told him to. We must all give thanks that he did. Jeff's passion was for families who have children with special needs. He founded a ministry catering to the needs of these families. But what most of you do not know is that Jeff was attacked physically and mentally by the Devil for these efforts.

I would tease Jeff that he was a modern-day Job. He gave all he had in this world to do God's will, and from that moment on, he was afflicted to the point of death. In May 2017, Jeff lost this battle. God saw his suffering and called him home after he had fought the good fight.

Through all his pain and suffering, he continued to provide for his family and the community he so dearly loved. He never let his afflictions keep him down for long. Once, when I sensed he was very discouraged, I took my Bronze Star and pinned it on his chest. He deserved it much more than I did.

Jeff, through all his afflictions, never lost sight of his God-given mission. He remained an obedient, selfless servant of God and his flock. The best way to honor the bravest man I ever knew is to continue what he started. We must be the men we need to be for our families and others who need us. I miss you, my friend, but I shall never forget. I will gladly pick up the standard you carried and continue to march up that hill.

PREFACE

To watch someone you love live his passion boldly is an awe-inspiring privilege, especially when he's fighting for his life as he does it. My husband's passion was to support and encourage the special-needs community—in particular, dads who have children with special needs. Jeff's life was committed to helping fathers stay in the game. It grieved him that so many dads walk away from their families after a diagnosis. That reality kept him up at night. He felt he had to do something, something essential to change the course of the future for these families.

In the spring of 2017, Jeff signed a contract with Kregel Publications. He was honored and overjoyed at the prospect of having this platform to speak directly to the men he knew were so in need of hope. His dream was coming true. Despite his own significant health issues, he was determined to make the most of this incredible opportunity. When Jeff passed away unexpectedly on May 23, 2017, one of my greatest fears was that his dream had died with him.

I am incredibly grateful to Jerold Kregel from Kregel Publications and Karen Neumair from Credo Communications. They held fast to the vision for this project and were unwilling to let it fade. They knew how important this book was to Jeff, and they believe in the critical need for this message.

I am also thankful to the amazing team of friends and special-needs dads from around the country who contributed to the book. Profound gratitude goes to retired Master Sergeant Rick Imel, one of Jeff's best friends and a fellow special-needs dad, who served as the military consultant and a contributor to the book. Thanks also to Eric Nixon, a volunteer with Joni and Friends Pennsylvania. He too was a friend to Jeff and is a fellow father of a child with special needs. His guidance and input throughout this process, and his significant contribution to "A Band of Brothers Study Guide" (see the appendix), have been invaluable.

This book is composed of Jeff's writings, public messages, and personal notes, along with messages from other dads on the front line. I have also included some personal letters of encouragement to the troops. It has been a source of comfort and healing to me during this time of often unbearable grief to read Jeff's writings and be reminded of what an amazing husband and father he was. Jon Alex and I live in the legacy of his love for us.

One of the things I always appreciated about Jeff was his willingness to be transparent about his own shortcomings and truthful about how raw and challenging life can be. He didn't try to sugarcoat the facts. He wrote openly about his own mistakes and what he had learned from them. You will find these hard-fought lessons in this book.

Jeff would often say about being the father of a child with profound special needs, "I am not the dad I thought I would be, but I am becoming the dad God wants me to be." It is my hope and prayer, just as it was his, that this book will be life changing for you and your family. May it help you thrive as the dad God has called you to be, and may you bravely lead your family to greatness.

Blessings from the Homefront,
Becky Davidson

INTRODUCTION

Shock and Awe

I wasn't ready to be the father of a child with special needs.

Who is ready?

One moment I was an up-and-coming thirtysomething whose life was aligning with the American dream, just as planned. I had a happy marriage, a successful career, and a new home, and my wife and I were expecting our first child. Everything was on track for the future I had imagined.

Then my world exploded.

We celebrated the birth of our "perfect" son—only to realize, as the months passed, that things weren't as perfect as we had thought. Little by little, a heartbreaking reality took shape. Our son wasn't achieving typical milestones. He wasn't developing as expected. One doctor visit led to three. Eventually a diagnosis was made, and then another and another. Finding out that our son would face lifelong, profound special needs was my own personal Hiroshima.

Everything I had hoped for, dreamed about, and so strategically planned was blown to bits. I realized that nothing about raising my son was going to be as I had expected—no playing catch in the backyard, no training wheels or bike rides, no shooting hoops in the driveway after dinner, no vacations to the beach, no University of Tennessee football games enjoyed together—nothing I had envisioned.

"Shock and awe" is a modern military strategy designed to render an opponent utterly powerless. The goal is to paralyze your adversary with overwhelming power and staggering force. This tactic overloads their will, perception, and understanding to such a degree that they are unable to fight back and can be easily overtaken.[1]

My son's diagnosis landed squarely on my heart with shock-and-awe impact. I was torn apart mentally and emotionally. I was powerless and easily overtaken by grief and fear. It would take years for me to get my bearings, accept my mission, and engage the fight, but I did so—and so can you.

Your journey as the dad of a child with special needs will be as unique as you are.

Your journey as the dad of a child with special needs will be as unique as you are, but maybe your world has been torn apart too. Maybe your dreams have been shaken, and you're not sure how you feel. Maybe you don't feel anything at all, and if you do, you're hesitant to express your feelings in words.

You probably find that your thoughts are a turbulent concoction of fear, disappointment, and even rage. You have difficulty focusing. Some days you teeter on the edge of freaking out. Other days you want to crawl into a cave and escape.

Maybe you're angry, but you're not sure who you should be angry with. Maybe you're afraid. Mostly you're overwhelmed, disappointed, frustrated, and confused. I would bet you feel pretty alone right now. How do I know?

Because that's exactly how I felt when I was drafted for this mission. I found myself caught in the middle of a conflict I never dreamed I would have to engage. I had no idea I had been specifically *chosen* for this assignment. I had no idea there was a plan and a purpose in all the chaos. I had no idea that one day I would recognize that my son with special needs was the best gift I had ever been given.

I've been a special-needs dad for almost twenty years now. I feel like a pro. But I was an absolute disaster of a dad in those early years. I'm not proud of that, but I am grateful that the grace of God transformed me and turned me into a warrior for my son and others with special needs. For years I asked God to change my son and heal him. In his sovereignty God decided instead to use my son to change and heal *me*.

I lived in denial and anger for the first couple of years. Honestly, I almost let our circumstances destroy me. You are going to be tempted to go down that road as well. It's a wide, beckoning road, and it's very easy to travel—but don't. It is an endless circle going nowhere.

You're a man, so your natural first response has likely been, "I can fix this." That's what I thought too. I became obsessed with problem-solving. I was too busy "fixing" my son to be his father. But the truth was that he needed a dad, not another therapist. I beg you, don't take that road. Trust me—I tried to navigate it, only to discover that it's a complete dead end.

If your journey is anything like mine, you're already shaken, so let me give you one thing to focus on now. There will be time later to deal with everything else, but let's start with the one thing that will matter most.

To be a successful dad to your child with special needs, you must wholeheartedly accept your mission.

Your mission is this: embrace your child exactly the way God created him or her. Love your child unconditionally and passionately, with all your heart.

Here is what I have learned: if you want to determine the depth of a father's strength, you must measure the depth of his heart for his child.

You have been drafted to father a unique child, and there is much to learn. As a special-needs dad, you need to know some rules of engagement. Let them sink in because they're opposite from what you might expect. You'll find that life with a nontypical child often requires you to unlearn typical ideas.

The Rules of Engagement

Your strength will be most magnified by your surrender.
Your toughness will be displayed through your tenderness.
Your significance will be measured by your selflessness.
Your success will be determined by your sacrifice.

You have a choice, Dad. You can flounder, stuck in anger, denial, blame, and an obsession to fix the brokenness, as I did, or you can embrace the brokenness with unconditional love. That's what God does for us. God takes the brokenness in our lives and from it creates beautiful gifts that he then uses to reveal himself.

Can I tell you a little about my own journey?

As I have said, I was a heartbroken young father in the early days. During that time, I had an encounter with God. Eighteen nights in a row, I walked down the street to a willow tree by a creek in our neighborhood. For eighteen nights I raged at God. I shouted at him, accused him, and even questioned whether he existed. For eighteen days I cried. God had defied my plans, my dreams, and my prayers by giving me a son with profound special needs. I was convinced that he had wrecked me and ruined my life. Like so many other dads in this situation, I took refuge inside a cyclone of my own anger, frustration, and denial.

Then one night, through tears of desperation, in a moment of stillness and clarity, the Holy Spirit whispered, "I've given you a blessing. What you do with the blessing is up to you."

Almost twenty years later, I now realize what God was trying to tell me. I thought that being a father to my son would be a burden and a hardship to be endured, but it's a mission, a purpose, and a blessing. The same is true for you and your child.

You've been given a gift. What you do with it is up to you.

The world looks at my son and sees a nonverbal young man crippled by cerebral palsy, intellectually disabled, and profoundly affected by autism. The world sees a boy who can't walk, talk, or function independently.

I don't see that. I see a beautiful masterpiece.

I see a tapestry of God's grace, God's beauty, and God's love woven together in a humble child. The world sees paint on damp plaster. I see the ceiling of the Sistine Chapel. The world sees a broken boy. I see Michelangelo's *David*.

The world sees a damaged human being. I see God's magnum opus.

God takes broken things and uses them to reveal himself to the world. It's true that his ways are not our ways. God has used my son to teach me the essence of unconditional love. God has used my son to show me how to embrace my own brokenness and accept my vulnerabilities. God has taught me that I don't have to understand him completely to obey him fully. God has shown himself to me and demonstrated the essence of our father-son relationship through my experiences as a dad to my own son. And he will do the same for you.

Our life has been excruciatingly difficult at times. We have suffered more challenges than we could ever have anticipated or imagined. We have cried oceans of tears and battled the deep waves of anguish. We have ached in our despair and wallowed in the dark pit of hopelessness.

We have questioned God, doubted God, and pleaded with God.

Despite all of that, today we stand certain of one truth: God hides beauty in brokenness. This is part of the mystery of God. Your child is perfect, and so is mine, because God creates nothing but masterpieces.

"For we are God's handiwork, created in Christ Jesus to do good works, which God prepared in advance for us to do" (Ephesians 2:10).

The call to be the dad of a child with special needs isn't an easy one; in fact, it's a highly classified mission for which only the elite are chosen. If you've been chosen, then you're honored to be graced by God himself.

In my home I have a living picture of how God uses the ordinary for the extraordinary. In my son I have a living, breathing temple of the Almighty—a window into the heart and soul of God.

Now I understand what God meant when he said he had given me a blessing. My prayer is that this book will help you realize that you too have been given a treasured gift in your child with special needs. Not only is your child a gift, but God has placed you on a specialized mission. You have a new purpose and a new destiny. You're a soldier in an essential army—and you have what it takes.

Let me share with you what God has taught me. Let me help train you to be a part of this army. Together we can change the world and speak up for those who have no voice. Together we are brothers in arms.

CHAPTER 1

Drafted

"I want you."
UNCLE SAM

When were you drafted? Was it the day your child was born, or did you come to the realization a bit later, as I did? When Jon Alex was born, we rejoiced, as all parents do. We celebrated the arrival of our firstborn child, a son! I remember looking down at his tiny face and feeling such incredible pride and joy. I was flooded with anticipation of our future together. This was my little guy, and we were going to be the dynamic duo. I would coach his Little League baseball team, just as my dad had coached me. We would play basketball together and go on great adventures to remote places. I would teach him to shave, drive, and make great barbecue. He might even ask me to be his best man, just as I had asked my father. My heart was overflowing with hope and expectation.

Not long after our son was born, however, it became clear he had some developmental issues. Over time we saw more and more concerning indicators. Eventually he was diagnosed with autism, cerebral palsy, and epilepsy. Although I didn't know it at first, I had been drafted to be the father of a child with profound special needs. I didn't have a clue what that might mean. I didn't understand anything. In time I would come to consider being drafted the greatest honor of my life, but I didn't know that in those early years. It felt like I'd been cheated out of my dreams. To be honest, I didn't handle it well.

How are you doing?

Seriously, how are you holding up?

I want to be honest with you right from the start. Being drafted is, by nature, something that happens to you without your expressed consent. It happens *to* you. In other words, you didn't pick this. The trouble with things you don't pick is that they can easily become things you resent. This is a tricky path to navigate unless you have some help. When I was new to this, there wasn't much help out there, and dads were walking away from their posts in droves. That trend is still in effect—and it has to stop.

I'm writing this book because I don't want you to be one of those dads. I'm going to tell you the truth about my journey, the places where I almost lost it, the depths of my despair, and the path to victory. You've been drafted, and nothing can change that, but how you respond has everything to do with your ultimate success.

DECISION TIME

When a man is drafted, he is being called up into a bigger story. His own life is put aside for the sake of joining forces for the greater good. No one is drafted to fight alone. The transition from draftee to soldier is dramatic. To become a soldier, a man undergoes a radical transformation. He sheds his old clothes, his old way of life, and even his hair, and takes on a new identity. Much of the new identity is first established in basic training because that is where he learns how to think, talk, and act like a soldier.

I'm not going to ask you to shave your head, but I am going to ask you to begin to let go of things in your head such as expectations you have had about how your life was going to go. I am asking you to let yourself imagine what life could look like if you become a well-trained soldier in service to your family and a community who desperately needs you. This book is designed as a guide and basic training manual to help you. If you use it, you will find yourself better equipped for what lies ahead. You will also be more likely to find a "band of brothers." We cannot fight this battle without friends in the foxhole. Having other men in your life who get what you are going through is essential to your success.

Becoming a soldier is no small thing, as any military man can tell you. It will push you beyond what you think you can bear and demand everything you've got, but you will be the better for it, and so will the people you are fighting for. You have been drafted, and you must decide how you will respond. Before basic training begins, you will have to deal with the reality of your situation and how you are coping. We are going to look at the typical responses to being drafted. Only after you have dealt with these concerns can you fully accept your mission and become a soldier . . . so let's get moving!

IN THE BELLY OF THE BEAST

When I finally began to grasp the gravity of Jon Alex's disabilities and what they meant for our family, I was wrecked. I couldn't cope. In the interest of full disclosure, I felt as though God had ruined my life and had *purposed* to harm me. Realizing that my precious son would never walk on his own, speak, or live independently was a nuclear holocaust to my hopes and dreams. I was in the belly of the beast, and I had no idea how I would ever get out.

Any time you suffer a significant loss, even the loss of hopes and dreams, there is grief to deal with. For most of us a diagnosis of special needs is an automatic loss. Our hopes and dreams for our child have been compromised, if not destroyed.

Are you feeling that loss? Have you allowed yourself even to think about it?

I'm going to walk you through the stages of grief and how they presented in my life. I share this with you for one very specific reason: our culture tells men they can't and shouldn't *feel*. We're shamed and discouraged from showing emotion, and that lack of emotional expression can make us seem less human. Suppressing feelings is like ignoring cancer. It eats away at you until your natural, God-given feelings slowly begin to wither. It's essential for your success as a special-needs draftee to address your emotions. Don't be ashamed of *anything* you feel.

Disappointment, humiliation, guilt, rage, an uncontrollable need to fix the situation, depression, hopelessness, loss of faith, loss of drive and focus—these are normal reactions to profound grief. If any of these feelings don't apply to you, consider yourself fortunate; if they do—as I suspect may be the case—then stick with me.

> How long, LORD? Will you forget me forever?
> How long will you hide your face from me?
> How long must I wrestle with my thoughts
> and day after day have sorrow in my heart?
> How long will my enemy triumph over me?
>
> Look on me and answer, LORD my God.
> Give light to my eyes, or I will sleep in death,
> and my enemy will say, "I have overcome him,"
> and my foes will rejoice when I fall.
>
> But I trust in your unfailing love;
> my heart rejoices in your salvation.
> I will sing the LORD's praise,
> for he has been good to me.
>
> (Psalm 13)

Elisabeth Kübler-Ross was a Swiss-born psychiatrist who pioneered studies in dying and, in 1969, wrote the groundbreaking book *On Death and Dying*. It was in this book that she first discussed the now-famous five stages of grief—denial, anger, bargaining, depression, and acceptance. Her research suggests that many people pass through these stages at some point, but not necessarily in this order. These stages are very similar to what I experienced working out my own grief. Knowing what the stages are can help you better understand your feelings and what to do with them. I recognize that feelings can be tricky business for guys, but here's what I can tell you: *you can't be real if you don't know how you feel.* And you have to be real in order to be who God designed you to be. It isn't feelings that are the problem but trying to pretend to be a real person without knowing your own heart.

After almost twenty years as a special-needs dad with a career in special-needs ministry, I am much more attuned to my feelings than I was in those early months and years, and I understand my emotions far better than when I first started. I can readily grasp the inner workings of my heart now. I can also see the suppressed emotions in so many dads who are just starting this journey. When we don't proactively deal with our emotions, this repression can cause irreparable damage to our families. Our emotions are telling us something vitally important, so we must confront them in a godly way throughout this mission.

I realize that we're all coming to this battle from different places and with different backgrounds and experiences. Maybe your situation is unique. Maybe you have a child who defies current medical knowledge. Maybe your child is higher functioning and closer to typical. Maybe you have been able to accept your child's diagnosis. If you have waited years to have a child and have finally seen the realization of that dream, you may view this assignment differently. It isn't wrong to have different feelings and responses from the ones I had. It's only wrong to be less than real.

I want you to complete this training manual with me, even if your story is different from mine. I want you to become part of a movement of men who are showing up to their lives as special-needs dads—men who are leaning on each other and finding hope and courage together. Men who are telling the truth about their lives—the good and the bad. Men who are real. Men who are strong. I am inviting you to fight alongside brothers who know what it's like to be a member of an elite group: common men with an extraordinary call.

THE FIVE STAGES OF GRIEF

"No one ever told me that grief felt so like fear."

C. S. LEWIS

Denial: If You Don't Say It, Then It Isn't Real

My denial was so deep that I refused to say the word *autism* for three years after Jon Alex was diagnosed. I told myself I didn't want to accept any label put on my son, but in reality, I didn't want to believe his diagnosis might be accurate and think about all that this would mean for our family. I was terrified to let him be defined by some medical moniker, but even more, I dreaded facing the truth that my son wasn't going to be who or what I had expected.

I remember desperately clinging to the words *developmental delay* because they implied a time would come when his development would catch up. Those words were the anchor of my hope. But as my son got older, the gap widened instead of narrowing. Our "normal" was constantly being modified and adjusted. Every month we would reassure ourselves that Jon Alex would catch up, but with each missed milestone, our hope took another hit. It was a losing game.

I couldn't believe that I would never hear him say, "I love you," never hear him call me Dad.

I couldn't accept that my son would remain nonverbal his whole life. I couldn't believe that I would never hear him say, "I love you," never hear him call me Dad. It was a loss I could not calculate. How would he let me know when he was hurting? How would I know what he needed?

I couldn't accept that Jon Alex would never be able to walk independently, or that we would have to feed him every meal by hand. I couldn't grasp that I would never get another good night's sleep because his sleep patterns were so unpredictable. I shut my eyes to the truth that he would always need our help with everything: bathing, dressing, shaving . . . all his basic needs.

I was in full-blown denial, but denying the truth doesn't change the reality. Jon Alex was my son, and by refusing to accept him just as he was, I wasted time I could have used getting to know him better.

I stuck my head in the sand to avoid seeing and accepting the obvious. I hid from the truth in plain sight. I hid behind my desk, wrapped up in my job. I justified my choice, believing that I was doing what is required of a dad: working to provide for my family. But that was just an excuse.

My wife, Becky, would have to call down to my basement office to tell me she and Jon Alex were headed to bed because I would hide out until bedtime. I'm not proud of that, but it's the truth. I wasted time in denial because I didn't embrace what was. I wanted to hold on to my hopes and expectations instead of accepting what God had given me. It was a fool's errand, but it was all I knew to do.

It is completely normal to need time to let the truth of your situation sink in. It is right to expect it to be a process to assimilate your reality, but it is not okay to disengage because you are afraid to face the truth. It is not okay to pull away just to protect yourself.

You are the leader of your family. If you hide, there will be no one for them to follow. *You* are the standard bearer—the soldier who carries the flag of your unit, your regiment. That flag leads the troops into battle. It shows everyone which direction to go, and it infuses them with courage! That's what you are for your family, but if you hide, they'll be left in confusion and will have to make their own way.

Denial Checklist

Here are some signs you might be stuck in denial:

- You're anxious, easily irritated, intolerant, and frustrated. Your mind knows something is wrong, and it's trying to tell you there's something you need to work out (like that annoying gravel in your shoe).
- There are topics you refuse to talk about.
- You might acknowledge that there's a problem, but you feel powerless to do anything about it.
- You work hard to change circumstances you have no control over, but you ignore what you can change.

- When confronted about yourself, you deflect or project the problem onto others.

Dad, I encourage you to surrender your pride and give your disappointment to God. Ask him to help you see your child and his or her disability as an opportunity and to give you a new identity as a special-needs dad. Ask him to help you love your child the way he does. Ask God to help you accept the gift you've been given.

God helped me accept my child's disabilities and my new reality, but it took a long time. When I finally accepted the truth, our world shifted, and life became easier. I was no longer fighting what was. Instead, I learned to welcome what could be. I don't want you to suffer and cling to denial like I did, so I offer this prayer for you:

> Father, thank you that this man is here and willing to ask for the truth to be revealed to him. Please show him what he needs to see. Show him what a gift his child is and how lucky he is to be drafted as a special-needs dad. Be strong for him and help him be a righteous standard bearer for his family. Reveal to him the brave warrior you have made him to be. Amen.

Anger: Where There's Anger, There's Pain

Anger was the first emotion I felt when this journey began. I was angry, and I wanted someone to blame. Who caused this? Why had this happened? How could something like this be happening to us? Denial quickly followed because to face the magnitude of how all this was going to change my life was simply too much. I danced between anger and denial for years, and, oh, how I wanted someone to blame for my pain.

Maybe you don't feel angry. Maybe you feel frustrated, irritable, or like every day is a bad day. All these feelings can easily disguise anger. If you did not grow up in a home where emotions were allowed, then you may not have any idea what anger really feels like.

If you were not allowed to be angry, then you might have learned to use frustration to cover your anger.

Anger Checklist

Anger is almost never a primary emotion (meaning that it's a warning sign, not a root problem). It's a reaction to mask fear, hurt, and our need to avoid guilt or shame. We often feel angry to cover an unbearable sense of our own vulnerability. Here are some red flags to look for:

- You find yourself blaming and attacking people, especially your spouse.
- You use silence and distance as tools to keep other people away.
- You mull over the times you've been wronged and refuse to let them go.
- Your feelings smolder under the surface and erupt without much control on your part.
- You secretly feel bad about things you've said when you were stressed.
- People don't readily share their feelings or concerns with you for fear of how you may respond.
- Your mood makes people feel tense, as though they're walking on eggshells.
- You have forgotten how to have fun.

I made the near-fatal mistake of letting anger and denial destroy me in the early years of our son's life. I acted out of my anger and let it affect my relationship with my wife, family, and friends. I mulled over how I had been cheated. I felt robbed of so much . . . and I was furious. I fantasized about building a massive bonfire of baby milestone books and hosting a giant book-burning party. I would invite all the parents of children with special needs to throw their milestone books on the fire too as it stretched out toward a bloodred sky. We would feel the glow of the fire against our faces as we shook our fists and raged at an unseen God.

I was angry at life and furious with God. It was a bitter time. That's the thing about anger. It's a reasonable and appropriate response to feeling betrayed and disappointed, but if you hold on to it for too long it becomes corrosive. Anger is a warning sign. It's supposed to alert you to the fact that you've been hit. Somewhere inside you there's pain. You've been hurt. Anger tells you there's something deeper going on. If you refuse to dig beneath the anger to unearth the root of the problem, it will eat you alive. Unresolved anger becomes bitterness, and bitterness is incredibly dangerous. Sadly, I've seen some special-needs dads who've never gotten over their initial anger, and life has not gone well for them.

So what do you do? If you find yourself unable to loosen your grip on anger, you have to go to God. Ask him to show you what you're really angry about and help you resolve the issue.

Don't be ashamed of your anger; it reflects how much you care, but don't mistake anger for power. I have seen many men throw around their anger to intimidate and control other people. Anger isn't a joystick you can use to control your world. It's a tool meant to help you cope with overwhelming feelings. Surrender and confess your anger to God. Ask him for help. Don't let anger rob you of your joy, peace, and contentment.

Anger also becomes one of the biggest obstacles in our relationships with our spouses. Men tend to transfer or direct their anger toward their wives and other family members, lashing out with predictable results. If you aren't careful, anger will rob you of any hope of a positive relationship with your children. It can destroy your marriage and family life. We must realize early in this journey that men and women grieve differently. We must allow room for that difference and understand that we may not be at the same stage as our spouse or children. Again, I have seen more special-needs dads destroyed by their inability to let go of anger than perhaps anything else. Be aware of your unchecked anger!

This is my prayer for you:

> Wise Father, you created us with powerful emotions. You gave us anger for a reason. Your Word tells us to be angry but not to sin (Ephesians 4:26). Help this man find the root of his anger. Help him see his pain and give that pain to you. Give him the courage to let go and move on to life and hope. Direct his path. Lead him to freedom. Amen.

Bargaining: The Great If/Then

In our brokenness and desperation, we can find ourselves trying to negotiate with God. I remember in the early days telling God that if he would just heal my son, I would go all over the world sharing the amazing story of his faithfulness. I really thought I could make a deal with God. Many of us, in our most desperate moments, try to conjure up some magical way to change our circumstances. We feel trapped and think we can orchestrate a way out.

Bargaining as a stage doesn't often last long, but it's an important part of the process of moving through grief. If you're bargaining, then part of you is settling on the fact that your circumstances are out of your control. The most important part of this process is to admit that you have *no* control over the circumstances surrounding your child's condition. If God doesn't respond to your offer to trade, you have no other option but to accept your circumstances for what they are. The irony is that there is power in doing just that! To accept what *is* allows us to be present, connected, and engaged with what is real.

Do you believe God is working all things together for your good? This is where the rubber meets the road.

When we pass beyond bargaining, we see our situation in terms of what *can be* instead of what needs to change. Our prayers become more about asking God *to use* our circumstances than *to change* them. If God doesn't respond to our cries for change, then we must accept that he has a plan to use this struggle for our benefit. We can know that he not only will walk with us through it but will ultimately work it out for our good (Romans 8:28).

One of the toughest things you need to determine is what you believe about God. Do you believe God is good? That he has your best interest at heart? Do you believe God is working all things together for your good? This is where the rubber meets the road.

If God is who he says he is, then we must accept that whatever he says is true. *You are* loved by God. You matter to him—infinitely so. God cares deeply about what you're going through. He cares so much that he wants to go through it *with* you. Make the decision to believe him. Settle your mind on it. If he is for you, and your circumstances don't change, then there's purpose in what he's allowing in your life. Get on the same page with him, and you'll find that there's a lot less frustration and resistance in your life. Fight him, and you'll find your very existence unbearable.

God's Word tells us, "Know therefore that the Lord your God is God; he is the faithful God, keeping his covenant of love to a thousand generations of those who love him and keep his commandments" (Deuteronomy 7:9) and "The Lord your God is with you, the Mighty Warrior who saves. He will take great delight in you; in his love he will no longer rebuke you, but will rejoice over you with singing" (Zephaniah 3:17).

Bargaining Checklist

You know when you're bargaining with God, but you may not realize what bargaining says about you. Ask yourself these questions:

- What is it I really want?
- Do I know what's best for me/us/our child, or do I just want relief?
- What do I really believe about God?
- Can I trust God even if he doesn't do what I want him to?
- Is it possible that my situation is actually designed to bring me closer to God?

> Lord, help this man settle in his heart that you are for him. Help him to know to the marrow of his bones that you care for him and mean him no harm, only good. Amen.

Depression: The Dark Night of the Soul

We're all familiar with sadness. We know what it means to be brokenhearted. When we are grieving, it's totally normal for us to feel overwhelmed by sadness. Some men respond to this by withdrawing and becoming very quiet. They don't feel like talking and don't want to be bothered with questions about how they're doing. Men don't generally show or share feelings easily. We learn to hide our emotions as a sign of personal strength. We love to feel as though we're in control. The problem comes when the sadness persists and isn't dealt with. It can all too easily become full-blown depression. I know because I have struggled with this myself.

In addition to handling Jon Alex's profound special needs, I have also experienced life-threatening health issues. I have battled one dark day after the next and have experienced loss after loss, including the loss of my foot. I haven't been able to drive for several years, and I find myself in the demoralizing position of having to depend on others for the simplest of daily needs. I know how tough life can get.

As a soldier, it's important to know when you are safe and when you need to call for backup. Usually sadness can be managed with time, self-care, truth, and some mental toughness. What I mean is that with the passing of time, some attention to our own emotions, a firm grip on the truth of God's Word, and some mental fortitude, sadness will typically pass on its own. However, depression is a different matter. If you are depressed, you need backup. How is depression different from sadness?

When we're experiencing sadness, painful feelings usually come in waves, mixed with times of joy or happy memories. When experiencing depression, we tend to stay down for an extended period. Depression, unlike sadness, also robs us of our self-esteem. If you're sad, you typically still feel fundamentally okay about yourself, but with depression you can struggle with a sense of worthlessness or even self-loathing. With sadness you can cheer up, but with depression it seems nothing can lift your spirits. Sadness and depression can overlap, but depression is usually accompanied by a sense of defeat.

Depression Checklist

People who are experiencing depression may feel or exhibit the following:

- Lack of interest and pleasure in daily activities
- Significant weight loss or gain
- Insomnia or excessive sleeping
- Lack of energy or inability to concentrate
- Feelings of worthlessness or excessive guilt
- Recurrent thoughts of death or suicide[2]

It's important to remember that being depressed doesn't mean you're less spiritually mature or less of a man. Many faithful men of God have struggled with depression, including Moses, Job, David, and Jeremiah. Being depressed doesn't disqualify you from being a man after God's own heart.

Depression can be very serious. It's vital for the success of your mission that you know your own heart. If you don't, you can spend years simply trying to survive something you can't control. Be brave and get honest with yourself. Are you sad? Are you depressed? Ask the Lord to help you discern the difference and to lead you if you need to seek help. There's never any shame in calling for backup. It's wise to know what you need and to ask for it.

> Father, give this man a clear understanding about what is going on in his heart. Shine your light on his grief and give him wisdom to know when he needs help and the courage to ask for it. Be his joy and restore his hope. Amen.

Psalm 34:18–19 assures us that "the Lord is close to the brokenhearted and saves those who are crushed in spirit. The righteous person may have many troubles, but the LORD delivers him from them all."

Acceptance: It Is Well with My Soul

When I finally came to accept Jon Alex's profound disabilities and what they meant for our lives, everything changed. This milestone brought about a palpable shift for our family. I saw with new eyes what could be. With acceptance, I was giving God the leeway he needed to teach me what my role would be and to show me our future. Life made more sense as I embraced my responsibility as a warrior for my family.

If you're struggling to accept your role as a special-needs dad—if you feel cheated out of life or robbed of your dreams—I can't encourage you enough to work through your feelings and give God a chance to speak hope to you. Acceptance isn't the same as resignation; on the contrary, it's a powerful, positive act of the will. Acceptance is a choice you make to refuse to argue with what is. Acceptance says yes to what is happening right now.

When God appeared to Moses in the burning bush, he used the name "I AM" to identify himself as the God of Israel, the same God who appeared to Abraham, Isaac, and Jacob (Exodus 3:14). I love that God calls himself "I AM." Simple as this may sound on first hearing, it's a strong declaration. If you want to be with God, you must be present in the life he has assigned you. You can only be with God in the *now*. He didn't call himself "I was," as though he were living in the past, or "I will be," as though he would manifest himself at some point in the future. No, he is "I AM"—here and now, active and available in this present moment. If we want to be where God is, we must be present—available and fully yielded to him—in real time.

In this mission as a special-needs dad, you will feel an incredible temptation to try to escape the hardships of the assignment. You will want to run, to hide, and to check out—but don't. You will miss all the destiny and purpose that have been written into your story. Long before you were born, you were assigned good things to accomplish.

You were sent here to do specific things that only you can do. Don't second-guess God, as I did. Accept his call on your life and walk in the fullness of it: "Before I made you in your mother's womb, I chose you. Before you were born, I set you apart for a special work" (Jeremiah 1:5 NCV).

> Lord, help this man fully accept his reality. Help him see the purpose in his assignment and catch a vision for his mission. Draw him into this army of men who serve and protect the neglected and overlooked of this world. Help him see that you are here and that you long to walk every step of this mission with him. Amen.

Now here's the truth: it would be wonderful if you could deal with your grief once and have it over and done with, but that isn't the case. You will again and again be faced with situations that revive these old feelings. Your child gets a new diagnosis, you get another call from a frustrated principal, your friends are celebrating their kids' championship victory while your child has never thrown a ball—each time you'll have to reckon with your grief anew. When you find yourself there, come back to this chapter and read these words, turn to your friends for support, and ask God to meet you where you are. Each time you do, you'll get stronger and the downtime will get shorter. Each time you face this challenge, you're being given an opportunity to improvise, adapt, and overcome. You're becoming a soldier, and this is what we do.

A Story from the Front Line

Chad Quarles lives in Arizona with his wife, Staci, and their two daughters, Madelynn and Kayla. This is a personal story from his life on the front line.

We learned that our daughter Madelynn had a cyst in her brain during my wife's first ultrasound. What was supposed to be a joyous and memorable moment quickly turned out to be devastating and overwhelming. Over the next month I had a deep feeling of self-shame and responsibility. I couldn't help but replay all my old sins and wonder if they were the cause of my daughter's disorder, as though somehow my sins had finally caught up with me. This experience shed light on my inaccurate understanding of God's grace and Jesus's finished work on the cross. During that one month I determined to live as righteous a life as I could, hoping I could earn God's healing. I read numerous books and essays on healing and how to convince God to grant this blessing. These thoughts and efforts were baseless and fruitless, and through them God helped me understand the nature of grace.

My breakthrough moment occurred one evening as I was cleaning the gym floor in a local church. I had just purchased a portable radio and headset so I could listen to music while I cleaned. Over the course of several weeks, I tried to tune in to radio stations, only to be disgruntled that there was no clear reception in the building.

However, one evening my radio remarkably tuned in to a Christian station that was playing a sermon on John 9, the story of the man who had been born blind. The pastor spent much of the message explaining the question the disciples asked of Jesus: "Rabbi, who sinned, this man or his parents?" As he described the love and heart of God toward people impacted by medical disorders and disabilities, and how their lives could be lived daily for the glory of God, all my presumptions and guilt began to erode. This was the first moment since we had learned about our daughter's condition that I found hope and realized that God wasn't punishing our family.

MISSION CRITICAL

- ☐ Assess your current emotional condition.
- ☐ Surrender your pain to God.
- ☐ Choose to embrace your mission.

CHAPTER 2

Absent Without Leave

We need to settle something now, before we go any further. I need to know this.

What kind of man are you?

One of the greatest challenges a man will ever face is being confronted with a situation that leaves him feeling powerless. Men are great at defending their turf, problem-solving, and taking charge . . . that is, until we find ourselves caught in something over which we have no control.

What happens when a man feels defeated before he even starts?

He wants to retreat.

We love to be the heroes. We love to come through for people and to win! But what happens when we feel helpless? Helplessness is our kryptonite. We're supposed to be able to handle things—to have all the answers, to be able to fix it.

But what if it can't be fixed?

When we feel powerless, we have to dig deep. We have to decide who we're going to be. We must commit to showing up even when it seems too hard, because that's what soldiers do. They keep showing up, no matter how difficult the situation may be, until the job is done. When we feel helpless, we must exercise the one power we always have. We must take the action that can change everything.

THE CHOICE

Viktor Frankl was an Austrian-born Jewish physician and survivor of the Holocaust. In October of 1944 he and his wife, Tilly, were sent to Auschwitz concentration camp. Viktor was then moved to Kaufering, a camp in Bavaria, where he spent five months working as a slave laborer. He was later moved to another camp, where he served as a physician to inmates. During the war his mother and brother died in Auschwitz, and his wife died in a nearby camp. His pain and loss were seemingly unbearable, but what he learned from this experience still benefits us today.

After three years in concentration camps, watching men suffer dehumanization in the most gruesome of ways, Frankl was liberated by American soldiers. He had endured unthinkable hardship, grief, and trauma; he had lost his family and was stripped of his identity as a successful physician. In the end he would write an account of his experiences that still informs our thinking. In 1946, only one year after his release, he published *Man's Search for Meaning*, which highlighted what he believed to be the key to his survival.

Frankl believed that, even in our toughest moments, we have a choice as to how we will live. We can choose to live with purpose and intention . . . or not. He also noted that there are two kinds of men: decent and unprincipled. In the end Frankl suggested that a man can survive almost anything if he makes the choice to live decently and to search for meaning and purpose in his hardship.

He believed that we can choose our outcome by opting to embrace our struggle and learn from it. According to Frankl, the way a prisoner imagined his future affected his survival and longevity. He believed that it was important to envision one's future playing out in a positive and hopeful way and attributed much of his own endurance to having purpose. He saw himself surviving his horrible ordeal and bringing healing and hope to others. Frankl wrote, "Everything can be taken from a man but one thing: the last of human freedoms—to choose one's attitude in any given set of circumstances, to choose one's own way."[3]

Men, we cannot choose what happens to us, but we can choose how we respond. That's the one power no one can take from us. We decide three things:

- What meaning we will give a situation or event (Is it a blessing or a curse?)
- How much attention and energy we will devote to that situation
- How we will respond or react to any given situation

Our decisions play a huge role in determining our identity. If you want to succeed on this mission as a special-needs dad, you're going to have to decide what meaning you will give to this mission, how much focus and attention you'll give it, and how you will respond when things get tough. The choice is yours.

To put off deciding is to start going AWOL. The father who does this is physically present but not engaged with his family. He's likely a good guy who is overwhelmed and simply doesn't know what to do, so he makes the choice to avoid instead of engage.

Some men physically walk away from their families—they're deserters. That isn't who you are, or you wouldn't be reading this book. You want to do the right thing or you wouldn't be here, but you must watch out for the temptation to be *around* your family but not *with* them. Dads who go AWOL find ways to avoid being involved with their families. I'm not talking about a dad who is engaged but needs a break. It's vitally important for you to find ways to take breaks from the intensity of this life, but these breaks need to have purpose and be intentional. They need to refresh, encourage, and revitalize you to return to active duty on the front line.

When you start going AWOL, you avoid reality, just as I did. You haven't abandoned your family physically, but you leave them waiting for leadership and emotional connection. These dads give themselves permission to opt out of being involved by making excuses and avoiding close interaction with their families. You don't have to be a bad guy to go AWOL; you just have to close your eyes to how very much you are needed.

GOING AWOL

By all the usual measures, I was winning the game. Some would say I was running up the score.

A man defines himself by where he is in his career, how much he earns, and how favorably he compares to others. This is the way men are taught to keep score. We define and assess our strength by how we're doing as warrior, protector, and provider. That's our identity—our scoreboard. We're proud fixers. Give us any problem and we'll quickly present you with a six-part plan on how to solve it. So when we're faced with the challenge of parenting children with disabilities and the need to redefine our role as fathers, we're confounded.

The true measure of a man is how well he loves and serves his family and community.

The true measure of a man is how well he loves and serves his family and community. In Jesus's words, "The greatest among you will be your servant. For those who exalt themselves will be humbled, and those who humble themselves will be exalted" (Matthew 23:11–12).

His example, from beginning to end, was to humble himself and serve, even when this choice led to his death. Jesus relinquished the beauty and safety of heaven to be born into a broken and hostile world. He lived as a humble teacher and died between two thieves on a cross of shame. He was God but didn't consider that position, that distinction, something to cling to. He didn't hold on to an exalted image of himself but gave himself wholeheartedly to the people who needed him. Jesus came to us because he cares for us.

In Paul's words, "In your relationships with one another, have the same mindset as Christ Jesus: Who, being in very nature God, did not consider equality with God something to be used to his own advantage; rather, he made himself nothing by taking the very nature of a servant, being made in human likeness. And being found in appearance as a man, he humbled himself by becoming obedient to death—even death on a cross!" (Philippians 2:5–8).

This kind of sacrifice is hardly a popular concept, but it's what

Jesus did and what he hopes we'll do. He needs us to come through for the helpless and the weak.

When I was first confronted with the challenge of having a son with cerebral palsy and autism, I felt powerless. I immediately threw myself into the familiar role of provider. This is where I felt comfortable. I defined my role as father and husband by how well I was doing as the breadwinner. As long as I was financially successful, providing for my family, and advancing in my work, I was scoring points in my self-made system. I was successful. I was strong.

I was running up the score, yes . . . but playing on the wrong field.

It took time for me to find the right path, but eventually I made the choice to surrender my dreams, my plans, and my desires for my life to God's purposes. He chose me to be the father of a child with special needs because he knew I could do it. But I had to learn to do it his way. I had to learn to become a true servant to my family and community.

The more selfless I became, the more attuned I was to the needs of my wife and child. The more willing I was to lay down my life for my family, the more significance I began to have in their lives. Today I realize that the way I respond to being a special-needs dad and the sacrifices I'm willing to make in the best interest of my family are the true markers of my success. What God considers important is seldom what matters according to the world's standard.

The ability to thrive as a dad to a child with special needs is developed over time. Ultimately, such a father is involved, engaged, and passionately devoted to serving his family. He is focused on being a servant leader. He lays down his own dreams, plans, desires, and aspirations in order to fulfill God's calling on his life. He's like a well-trained warrior who knows he's a part of something much bigger than himself. He is on a mission—a player in a much bigger story.

Sound like a lot? It is, but it's also the way you become more like Jesus. Part of the gift of being entrusted with a child who has special needs is that God gives you a situation in which you *have* to trust him. You have to become more like Christ to handle the job. It's a tough assignment, but it has great rewards if you're only willing to show up!

You need to know that no one plans to go AWOL. No one wakes up and says, "This is the day I'll be checking out on my family." It happens over time, with each choice we make. A choice becomes a habit. A habit becomes a lifestyle. And a lifestyle crosses a line and becomes a reflection of our character. Without realizing it, and despite all the warning signs, we find ourselves absent without leave.

So how do you see this coming? What are the red flags? What choices or habits lead you down the path to becoming an absent dad? I have spent almost two decades watching men struggle with the temptation to go AWOL. I have, in fact, been that man. Over time I began to detect patterns in myself and others that were red flags. I started to recognize telltale signs.

Here are the top twenty-five warning signs that you may be going AWOL. You will experience some of them from time to time, but these shouldn't be your norm for relating to your family. Review these statements honestly and objectively. How you feel about the statements will tell you a lot about where you are on the journey. If you find yourself either offended or pricked in your conscience by what you read, it's most likely hitting a nerve.

TOP TWENTY-FIVE WARNING SIGNS THAT YOU MAY BE GOING AWOL

1. At home, surrounded by your family, you still find yourself daydreaming or thinking more and more about your work or hobbies.
2. You escape your home environment by spending most of your free time on television, the internet, a favorite hobby, video games, or social media.
3. You spend more time lamenting that your own needs and expectations aren't being met than you do serving the needs of your family.
4. You are reluctant to sacrifice your own dreams, ambitions, and plans to meet the needs of your family.

5. Your idea of expressing love for your children is to shower them with gifts and toys rather than to delight them by being engaged and interacting with them.
6. You can't remember the last time you spoke any words of affirmation or encouragement over your children. Most of your words are negative or discouraging.
7. You have accepted the role of protector and provider for your family and believe that should be enough to fulfill your role as a dad.
8. You rarely, if ever, pray over your children and family, calling down God's blessings, favor, and purpose over them.
9. You still think the story of your life is about you and that you are the main character in this story.
10. You let your anger, bitterness, or denial over your circumstances dictate your dealings, feelings, and actions toward your child.
11. You believe your role as a special-needs dad is more of a burden than it is a blessing.
12. You tend to gravitate toward your typical children at the expense of your child with special needs.
13. Your expectations for your relationship with your wife haven't changed even with the addition of a child with special needs into your family.
14. You are too obsessed with fixing your child to focus on the joys of fatherhood.
15. Your lack of understanding grace in your own life inhibits your ability to shower your child with unconditional love.
16. You are still letting your circumstances determine your joy and contentment, rather than discovering the gift you have been given in this child.
17. You are always comparing your life, your child, your family, and your circumstances to those of other people and continually lamenting the differences.
18. You don't believe your child is wonderfully made or created for a plan and a purpose, with a destiny to glorify God.

19. You spend more time asking God to change your circumstances than you do asking him to use your circumstances to teach you and reveal his presence to you.
20. You let your own pride, embarrassment, selfishness, and self-consciousness prevent you from talking or sharing about your child publicly or even from being seen around them.
21. You make excuses for and create busyness that prevents you from spending significant time engaged with your child.
22. You don't interact or engage with your child with special needs because you can't do so in the ways you were raised or have imagined.
23. You can remember the name, number, and position of every player on your favorite sports team but don't recall your child's birthday, teacher's name, favorite activities, or favorite books.
24. You feel that as long as you don't physically leave your family you aren't an absent dad.
25. You have read all twenty-four of these statements and have tried to make excuses to rationalize and justify your behavior about way too many of them.

As I said, in my early years I went AWOL myself.

I grew up the son of a basketball coach. I spent much of my youth either in a gym or on an athletic field. All my thoughts, dreams, and aspirations for my son were based on my own experiences. I wanted the two of us to play baseball together in the backyard and shoot hoops in our driveway. I bought a basketball goal before my son was even born so I would be ready.

My favorite childhood memories involved going to the University of Tennessee football games in Knoxville with my dad. We would leave early, listening to the pregame call-in show on the radio. We would be decked out in our orange and white clothes with our portable radios in our pockets.

We always ate barbeque for lunch at my dad's favorite place. We would arrive early to watch all the pregame activities and participate in all the game-day traditions. We would stand up and sing along to

"Rocky Top" a dozen times and collect souvenir cups on the way out of the stadium. My heart yearned to be able to carry on this family tradition by doing the same with my own son.

What about you? For some dads it's about music. For others it's about camping, boating, fishing, technology, or arts and science. We all tend to assume that we'll parent based on our own upbringing and memories. We make assumptions about the activities in which we'll engage with our kids.

When Jon Alex's disabilities became apparent, I didn't know what to do. I didn't know how to engage him, play with him, or interact with him at all. I felt helpless to know how to do anything with him that a typical father does.

My son is completely nonverbal, so I had no idea how I should talk to him. When I did attempt to engage him, I received no feedback at all. He couldn't walk, much less run or chase a ball. He was visually impaired and seemed to be in some distant, unreachable place. All I knew was that I was frustrated, depressed, and bitter over my circumstances. My coping mechanism was to avoid interaction altogether.

All of that changed in one night—in one holy, unforgettable, God-ordained moment.

Our son was around five years old, and I was sitting in my recliner, watching TV and unwinding after work. My wife was, as usual, multitasking. She was caring for our son, cooking dinner, and managing several other things at once. As part of our son's therapy, we hung a large platform swing from the ceiling in his room. Several times a day we placed him in that swing for a few minutes to stimulate his vestibular system. My wife asked whether I would at least swing Jon Alex for a few minutes so she could finish preparing our evening meal. Reluctantly I got up and took him into his bedroom to swing.

After a few minutes of silently pushing him, with my mind engaged in anything other than what I was doing, I quickly grew bored. Out of that boredom and for my own entertainment, I began adding sound effects every time I pushed his swing. At first I made the sound of a NASCAR race, then the sound of a fire truck.

Out of nowhere my son cackled.

I froze. What had just happened? I began making the sounds of airplanes, spaceships, and police sirens. My son was laughing, smiling from ear-to-ear and roaring with approval. The more feedback he gave me, the more determined I became to make him respond. All of a sudden we were playing together, and I was fully engaged—body, soul, and spirit.

In those minutes I realized my purpose and my mission. I delighted in bringing delight to my son.

In those minutes I realized my purpose and my mission. I delighted in bringing delight to my son. His smile and laugh were contagious.

All these years later, that hasn't changed. I delight in what delights my son. I have chosen to venture into his world rather than trying to lure him into mine. I have chosen to throw myself into whatever it is that brings him pleasure, not to try to coax him into doing what brings me pleasure.

Never was this more evident than one day last fall in the middle of football season.

I happen to believe that orange and white are the official colors of heaven. That's how passionate a fan of University of Tennessee athletics I am—especially when it comes to football. I bought my son his first Tennessee jersey before he was born and begged and cajoled my wife to let me decorate his room with some of my University of Tennessee memorabilia. I wanted to share this passion with my son, to experience the perfect day with him, just as I had with my own father growing up . . . but that wasn't to be.

One of the biggest games of the year for UT fans is when we play the University of Florida Gators. Ours is an intense rivalry that brings out strong emotions on both sides. Before the game, I was obsessed with the outcome. My friends and I discussed it, analyzed it, and made it our focus for days. I cleared my calendar for that

Saturday so I could watch on my big screen TV and pretend I was at the game. My wife was going to take care of our son and give me the gift of three uninterrupted hours of pleasure.

Then the phone rang.

One of Becky's best friends from out of town was visiting that day and wanted to have lunch with her—right smack in the middle of my beloved Tennessee versus Florida game. My choice was quite easy, actually. My wife lays down her life every day giving continuous care to our son. She rarely gets any kind of reprieve. She needed this lunch.

So I spent the time during the game wholly and completely engaged with my son. I fed him his lunch before moving him to the couch. For the next two hours, we played together. I sang over him. I scratched his back. I hugged him ferociously, and we just hung out. He is nonverbal, so I did all the talking. We played with a couple of musical toys he enjoys, and we had fun.

I thought for a second about the football game, but only for a second.

It isn't what you do with your children as a special-needs dad that matters. What matters is that you're fully engaged, fully involved, and fully committed to their welfare and pleasure. It's about being intentional with your time, not accidental.

At one point, with my arm over his shoulders, my son closed his eyes and took a brief nap. I sat on the couch with my heart full. I listened to Jon Alex's breathing as he slept. I told him, "You're safe here. No one can hurt you in my arms. I will love you forever. I'm so proud that you're my son. There's nowhere else I'd rather be and nothing else I'd rather be doing."

I realized that I'd been wrong all those years before. This *was* the perfect day. But it had taken me many years to get to that point. When I first realized how different my life would be as a special-needs dad, I truly struggled. The first time I went to an IEP meeting at school; the first time I shaved my adolescent son; the first time it sank in that he would never drive, marry, or have children—all those realizations left me struggling to make sense of my life.

Your life will never make sense to you until you realize and embrace the call God has for you as the dad of a child who has special needs. Only after I embraced my role and realized the gift God had given me did my own life start to make sense.

The truth is, before then I was a completely broken man. Not only was I broken, but I didn't even recognize the severity of my brokenness. When I looked in the mirror, I couldn't see my own emotional wounds. I had learned over the years to mask them from myself—unaware that they were visible to everyone else. I was living in denial about myself, incapable of finding any hope, cure, or solution to my problem on my own. I was helpless. I had a devastating heart problem, and I needed a miracle.

The bottom line is that I had spent my entire life living for myself. I was judgmental, hypocritical, and unloving to those who weren't like me. I had nothing to do with people who didn't look, act, think, vote, or believe like me.

I was selfish and overcome with pride. I measured success by the size of my house and the heft of my paycheck. All my goals and plans were wrapped in self-absorption. My life had been consumed by legalism, and my capacity to comprehend grace, much less offer it, had been shut down.

There had to be a bridge between who I was and who I wanted to be, but I was searching in all the wrong places. When you're broken inside, your life will be broken too. Have you ever noticed that the biggest blessings in life are so often concealed in the things you once considered burdens?

Love came down and rescued me. God sent a broken son into a broken world and to a broken father so we could together find God in our brokenness.

I prayed and prayed for God to heal my son. Then I realized that God had given him to me, "complete" with his profound special needs, in order to heal *me*. I suspect many parents of children with special needs will understand what I mean. We were chosen to be the trustees for some of God's most incredible gifts. As fathers, God has given us profound gifts in the form of our kids. God has designed us to be warriors, protectors, providers, encouragers, and equippers of our kids and our families.

I wish the younger, overwhelmed dad I had been could have been mentored and reassured in those early days by the mature, seasoned soldier I have become. It took me a while, but I eventually came to embrace all that this mission has to offer—and that has made all the difference. I would tell my younger self, as I tell you now, "This journey is going to be harder than you can imagine, but it's going to be one of the most richly rewarding experiences of your life." I would tell him, "There is purpose in the pain, a message in the mess, and every trial will produce triumph." I would counsel, "If you surrender your pain to God, then God will reveal himself to you in unspeakable ways."

Before we go any further, gentlemen, you need to decide here and now that you are going to be a committed dad. You need to declare war against any thought or idea that even begins to pull you away from your family. You must be courageous and strong. You have to decide.

> Dear Father, please help this good man fully commit to the life to which you have called him. Help him see who he really is and humbly ask for the help he needs. Give him hope in his heart and courage to overcome all obstacles. Amen.

A Story from the Front Line

Dave Bush lives in Pennsylvania with his wife, Sarah, and their two sons, Zak and Jacob. This is a personal story from his life on the front line.

When I was growing up, my dad went to work every day at our local Sears store, where he ran the automotive department. My early memories include going with my mom to pick him up from work on Fridays because she used the car that day. On Sundays, my brother and I went to church with our grandmother. Dad almost never went, but he was always at family dinner. After Sunday dinner, Dad would head back to his nine-to-five at Sears.

When I was about eleven, he lost his job. The store he worked for had downsized. The mall had arrived, and Main Street was becoming a ghost town. I remember my mother working two and three jobs and taking care of us while my dad "looked for work." As I recall, he would get a job only to lose it. My teenage memories of him consist of seeing him in his recliner in front of the TV, snacking and snoozing. There were times when I wished he would just leave. He, like lots of other guys in the 1970s and '80s, didn't know how to parent. He had other things to worry about or other things on his mind, so the full burden of parenting fell to my mother. My dad was a textbook absent dad. He was there but not there.

By the time I was old enough to get a job, all I wanted to do was work. When I first met my wife, Sarah, I was thirty-eight and single, with no kids and no life outside of work. Sarah had a five-year-old son named Zak who had special needs. I could see that he needed a dad badly, a dad who would be present, a dad who would be there for him. The struggle to be that dad has been difficult. I struggle daily to remain connected to a fourteen-year-old with autism who is my complete opposite, but I know that he needs me.

Shortly before my wedding I had a visit from my father, who told me something I had not heard since I was a little boy. He told me that he was proud of me. I was absolutely floored by this. It made me feel great. Now that I have been able to forgive my own dad for not having been there for me, I actually feel like a dad. Sarah and I also had a son we named Jacob, who is now six. These days the desire to go AWOL isn't as great because I am reminded that my fathers, both earthly and heavenly, love me and are proud of me. What would they think if I went AWOL on my boys?

MISSION CRITICAL

- ☐ Assess your potential to become an absent dad.
- ☐ Ask God to help you take your rightful place in your family.
- ☐ Ask friends for accountability.
- ☐ Surrender yourself completely to your mission.

CHAPTER 3

Basic Training

I have never had the honor of serving in the military, but I consider myself a patriot. I have a fierce love of country and a deep appreciation for all who have served to protect my freedom and that of my family. In my boyhood I would re-create battlefield strategies with my G.I. Joes. I would rain down terror on the enemy with tanks rolling and guns blazing. As I grew up, my fascination continued as I read accounts of great battles fought on foreign soil and of the brave men and women who gave all for the country they loved. Even now I look forward to opportunities to show my respect for those who have served this nation. It gives me great satisfaction to be able to buy a meal for a person in uniform or to show respect as veterans pass by in the local parade. I am passionate about this country and the men and women who have sacrificed to keep it free.

I have often wanted to create a way for new special-needs dads to be trained and prepared for their mission. My heart aches that we lose so many men in this battle, and I don't believe it has to be this way. I think that most of the time, dads feel overwhelmed and alone. They just don't know what to do. They feel inadequate and can't find their bearings, as though they've been caught in a firestorm without any backup.

For a man to try to navigate this struggle without a compass would be unwise and even dangerous. To face this challenge without support would be ill advised. He needs comrades, leadership, hope! If you're a new dad to a child with special needs or even a seasoned dad who is feeling lost, overwhelmed, or hopeless, or if you just want to be a stronger and better father, then embrace this training as though your life depends on it—because the success of your marriage and family just might!

YOUR ULTIMATE MISSION

In the introduction we touched on our mission; now it's time to dig deeper into the heart of the real call on our lives. After almost twenty years of fathering a son with profound special needs and helping other men in this community find their place as fathers, I am now convinced that one statement is at the core of everything we're called to do.

Your ultimate mission is this:

> Embrace your child with special needs exactly as God created him or her. Love your child unconditionally and passionately, with all your heart.

This is the cornerstone on which your life as a special-needs dad rests. Your ultimate mission is to give your child unconditional love and acceptance simply because they "are." I want you to think hard about this. Of all the men in the world, God chose *you* to father this special child. The Creator of the universe—the wisest, most infinitely loving being—looked at you and decided that you were worthy to care for his most beloved. You see, God himself hides in the broken and flawed things of this world. This is part of the mystery. He has a very special love for the people the world rejects.

When you lay down your agenda and your expectations for a typical life, you will realize that there is nothing your son can achieve that will ever make you love him more than you already do. You love your daughter simply because she is your child. This is the same kind of love God has for us. He loves and accepts us as is, just because we belong to him.

In my decades as a special-needs dad, I've come to treasure the sometimes small but exceedingly joyful moments this journey has had to offer. But to this day I still regret the early years when I allowed my anger, denial, and obsession with fixing my son to rob me of the sheer joy of just being his dad.

Eventually I came to understand the only statistic that really mattered. I realized I have *one* son, and he has autism. So I made a decision.

A choice.

I chose to love my son unconditionally just the way he is—with autism. I chose to embrace his differences, accept his challenges, and love him for who he is—my son.

I chose to engage with him without reservation or qualification.

Autism is just a label. Like the word *son*. The former word describes him, but the latter defines him.

Autism is just a label. Like the word *son*. The former word describes him, but the latter defines him.

Jon Alex is completely dependent on us for everything in his life. From the moment he wakes up until the moment he drifts off to sleep at night, we provide for his every need. He is incapable of surviving in this world without our full support. He is utterly helpless on his own. All throughout the day, I encourage him, affirm him, and express my unconditional love for him. I think about him all day long. I know his mannerisms and his needs so well.

I love him because he is my son. Not because he has done anything to merit or earn my love. In fact, there's nothing he could do or achieve that could make me love him more than I do. I believe in him despite his challenges. I embrace his differences, knowing that this is how he was created. I believe that he has been fearfully and wonderfully made, created for a plan and a purpose and destined to glorify God. He is my son, and I am his warrior, protector, provider, encourager, and equipper. God has called and equipped you to do the same for your family. You are your child's everything.

If you feel unable to meet this challenge, it's okay. Humble yourself, confess your need or lack, and ask God to help you love your family, especially your very special child, with his love. The truth is that none of us has enough love on our own. We are all selfish and small in our own strength, but Jesus came to make all things new. He will give you a new heart, a heart full of love for your child, if you'll only ask him.

BOOT CAMP

In basic training or boot camp, there are three distinct phases of instruction that correlate with the colors of the US flag: red, white, and blue. Recruits are received at their assigned post, and the transformation from civilian to serviceman begins. The typical life is cast off, to be replaced by a whole new identity. And so it is with us. When you're drafted to become a special-needs dad, you have to let go of "typical." That can seem nearly impossible unless you know you were meant for something more.

I think that I held on to my former life for so long because I did not have vision for my new role as a special-needs dad. That lack of vision made the struggle to embrace our anything-but-typical life so much more difficult. I want to challenge you not only to resist being an absent dad but to embrace with all your might this new assignment. You are now a soldier. You are fighting to defend and protect the neglected, forgotten, and dismissed of our society. You're called to lay down your life for them, to sacrifice for them, to give your all for them. This is the life to which you've been assigned, and just like a soldier in the US Army, you have a mission to fulfill.

"The true soldier," points out G. K. Chesterton, "fights not because he hates what is in front of him, but because he loves what is behind him."[4]

THE RED PHASE

In the red phase, soldiers learn the seven core values of the army. These are the very same values we need to embrace as special-needs dads: loyalty, duty, respect, selfless service, honor, integrity, and personal courage. These values are the plumb line for our lives. This is our code.

Loyalty

To bear true faith and allegiance to God, our marriage, and our children: this is the call of a special-needs dad. Loyalty is vital in any marriage, but never more so than in a family that faces great challenges. The demands and stressors of caring for a child with disabilities can put significant strain on this bond, so we have to be all the more focused and vigilant. We often face criticism and misunderstanding from outsiders as well. This means that our loyalty to our own "people" must be paramount.

As a Christian dad, you'll find that your loyalty to God will help you remain loyal and devoted to your family. Never underestimate how ready and willing God is to meet you in any challenge. Go to him with every concern and ask him to help you be a strong leader. If you feel your heart starting to stray, tell God the truth about how you're feeling. He will always be loyal to you.

When your allegiance to your family is obvious, your family feels safe. Your wife can relax and rest in the knowledge that you'll be there for her. Your kids will see your devotion to them and feel loved and secure. One of the best ways to develop loyalty in a family is to have fun together.

Here are some simple, practical ways to help your family develop a sense of oneness and fidelity.

Create a Family Motto

A motto can be anything you like, but it needs to bind you together. Some simple but effective examples: "We stick together." "One for all and all for one." "We love hard and play hard." "Whatever it takes."

Our personal family motto is "Chosen, Called, Committed."

Display your motto in your home and use it often to create unity and a sense of belonging.

Come Up with a Family Cheer!

A family cheer can be a fun way to pull everyone together. Throw a few simple moves into the mix to add some flair. The chant we adopted has been around for many years. It goes like this:

Everywhere we go
(echo) Everywhere we go
People want to know
(echo) People want to know
Who we are
So we tell them
We are the Davidsons
The mighty, mighty Davidsons

Your cheer can be one that builds up your family or just makes you laugh. No matter what it is, you can be sure it will tighten the bond between you.

Create a Mission, Vision, and Value Statement for Your Family

Your life has purpose. The life of your family does too. Make your mission statement simple, authentic, and easy to remember. Pull together a family meeting to come up with your statement, and then post it in a prominent place in your home.

Duty

Men, fulfill your responsibilities—there are no shortcuts! It's our duty as men and fathers to show up, both emotionally and physically, for our families. It's our duty to love our people well . . . and to love ourselves well too. We can't be the strong leaders our families need if we fail to take care of ourselves. We'll break down these responsibilities in detail in the coming chapters, but here is a summary. Your duties as a dad are to:

- Protect and defend
- Provide

- Strengthen
- Equip

Consider the impact on your family members if you successfully fulfill your duty to them. Just like a soldier, if you do your duty, lives will be saved and people preserved. If you don't fulfill your duty, the result can be disastrous. You are far more important than you realize.

Respect

Respect and dignity go hand in hand. How you feel about yourself will be reflected in the way you treat your family. If you disrespect your wife or kids, you weaken the entire foundation of your home. If you disrespect yourself, you do the same. Respect is at the core of Christianity. Jesus shared the heart of it in the Sermon on the Mount when he gave us what has come to be known as the Golden Rule: "So in everything, do to others what you would have them do to you, for this sums up the Law and the Prophets" (Matthew 7:12).

The heart of respect is to treat another person with the same grace, the same forgiveness . . . you would hope to receive yourself.

The heart of respect is to treat another person with the same grace, the same forgiveness, and the same kindness and goodness you would hope to receive yourself. It doesn't matter what they do or might deserve. We're called to live up to a higher standard.

So how do you show respect as a man, a husband, and a father? Respect begins with the way you treat yourself, then the way you treat others.

Have some dignity, men!

Act in a way that's worthy of who you are. You are the living temple of God. What you say, what you do, what you watch, and what you listen to reflect how much respect you have for yourself and God. Behave like a man of dignity and worth—because you are one. Your self-respect will then flow to your wife and kids. Do you want them to honor you? Do you expect them to respect you? Then conduct yourself in a way that warrants respect. Don't belittle or talk down to your children. Don't be weak and indifferent toward those in your own household. Even a child knows an imposter. Don't expect your wife or children to give you what you aren't willing to give them. Be strong and have courage. Lead with tenderness and kindness. Teach your children to respect you by showing respect both within and outside your home. Respect must be your standard.

It has been said that the best thing you can do for your children is to love their mother. Gentlemen, this is absolutely true. Let your children see how much you love your wife. Do things—even simple little things—to show her respect. Lift her up and encourage her. Compliment her in front of your kids. Be the kind of husband you want your son to be, because he's watching. Show your daughter what a good man looks like so she'll recognize one when she sees him.

No excuses, gentlemen! In this age of open disrespect, be a standard bearer. Hold up the flag of love so that others can follow.

Here are some practical ways to promote respect in your household:

- Listen carefully to your wife and children. One of the best ways to show someone respect is to listen to them intently.
- Value their input. Take to heart what your family members say. Show them you're listening by following through, by doing things they suggest or consider important.
- Treat everyone equally. It's easy to favor one child over another, especially in a special-needs family. Be sure all members of your family feel respected, equally valued, and loved.
- Show your wife honor by asking her opinion or showing interest in what is important to her. It's very easy to let your wife take on more than her fair share of family responsibilities because she has a natural tendency to rush in to care for everyone. It's

easy to turn a blind eye to family needs or claim we can't do things as well as she can. Take an honest look at the distribution of labor in your home. Are you showing respect to your spouse or hiding behind excuses?

- Make sure you're respecting yourself by using any free time you have to recharge and refuel in healthy ways. Free time is a luxury in a special-needs family. Use yours intentionally and carefully; make it really count. Your goal should be to recharge so you can then give your wife a reprieve. Respect each other's needs for rest and recovery. The battle takes its toll on both of you.

Selfless Service

Let me be frank. There is only one way to become a selfless servant—you have to die.

You owe it to God and family to lay down the comfortable life of getting what you want when you want it. Instead, ask God to infuse you with *his* love for your family. Let's face it, you don't have enough willpower on your own to live selflessly. No one does.

The welfare of the nation must be the primary concern of a soldier. In the same way, as a warrior for your family, your must focus your heart and mind on the ultimate welfare of your people. Only Jesus can help you put the well-being of your family above your own needs, but this is exactly what is required.

A well-trained soldier serving his country does so without any thought of recognition or gain. He will trudge through mud, sand, or snow for days, get by on little sleep or food for weeks at a time, suffer the loss of all personal comforts, and never complain . . . because that's his duty. So it is with us. We must show up for our families again and again, demonstrating absolute, selfless service with no expectation of reward other than the knowledge that God is proud of us. If we as men can do this for our country, how much more must we be willing to do so for our own flesh and blood?

If you don't feel you have the strength to accomplish this on your own, you're right! You must repeatedly ask God to help you—not only to show up but to follow through. If you don't have the desire to sacrifice like this but are willing to become willing, then ask for that desire. God will enable you if you're just willing. Selfless service is the way of Jesus.

Here are some ways to practice selfless service:

- Determine to make it your goal to outserve everyone else in your family.
- Offer to do things to relieve your wife without waiting to be asked.
- If you don't know how to provide some of the things your children need (for instance, you don't know how to do meal prep), then ask to be taught.
- Make sure everyone is cared for at the end of your workday before you take time for yourself.
- Encourage and appreciate your spouse even if she doesn't do the same for you. Lead by example!
- When you're tempted to complain or hide out, push yourself to show up strong, like a soldier on the battlefield would. This is your job.

Honor

The United States' highest military award is the Medal of Honor. This award is given to soldiers who make honor a matter of daily life. These soldiers cultivate the habit of behaving honorably and cement that habit with every positive choice they make. Honor is the act of believing and living out the values of loyalty, duty, respect, selfless service, integrity, and personal courage in everything you do.

It is our honor to serve our families. It's our honor and an act of worship to be a Christlike example every day. Make it your spiritual goal to live in such a way that you could receive a Medal of Honor from the Lord. He is the one you serve, and he is the one you should look to for encouragement and praise. Live so that one day you will hear from his lips the words, "Well done, good and faithful servant!" (Matthew 25:21).

To live an honorable life is to make a thousand little choices to live up to a higher standard than your flesh wants you to. This is a strategy of dying to yourself every day, but it's also a choice to show honor to others. How can you honor your wife and family?

Here are some practical ideas that are easy to implement and will go a long way toward showing honor:

- Watch your family carefully and call out what's good in them. One of the easiest ways to change the atmosphere in your home is to speak encouragement to those you love. This may be hard at first. You'll have to prime the pump before the words will flow. You can go a long way toward creating a healthy environment for your family by speaking blessings over them. The Bible says that the tongue has the power of life and death (Proverbs 18:21), so speak life over your people.
- Create awards for your wife and kids. Buy gum, candy, or some other small treats and reward people who are succeeding at the values you're trying to instill. The dollar store is a great resource for small incentives, and you can find printable award templates online. Just a little effort here can change the quality of life for everyone.
- If you want to honor your wife, ask her to teach you to take over one thing she is now responsible for. Maybe you can learn to manage your child's medications or fold laundry (a task easily done while watching TV). Taking something off her plate is a huge way to show her honor.

Integrity

To have integrity is to be honest, upright, and of high moral courage. Who do you know who has integrity? I always think of my favorite historical figures like Abraham Lincoln. Lincoln lived with such integrity that even today his honesty and moral courage inspire us. Lincoln once said, "I do the very best I know how—the very best I can; and I mean to keep doing so until the end. If the end brings me out all right, what is said against me won't amount to anything. If the end brings me out wrong, ten angels swearing I was right would make no difference."[5]

Also from Lincoln, "Adhere to your purpose and you will soon feel as well as you ever did. On the contrary, if you falter, and give up, you will lose the power of keeping any resolution, and will regret it all your life."[6]

Lincoln understood that his integrity was the most important virtue he possessed, and he wouldn't let it be compromised. Examples of this kind of integrity are harder to find these days, but that's all the more reason we need to be men who exemplify this character trait.

Here are some suggestions for walking as a man of integrity:

- Dig deeply into the Word of God and anchor yourself in truth. Let God's principles guide all your decisions.
- Create a list of qualities you believe are critical to your own integrity and live up to that list. (For example: I tell the truth. I don't compromise my relationship with my wife. I obey the laws of the land. I respect myself and others. I bow the knee to God alone.)
- Keep your focus on things that are hopeful and positive. Avoid negativity and drama.
- Be a man of your word. Do what you say you'll do, and keep your commitments. Be a man people can count on.
- Resist the temptation to compartmentalize your life. At times it's a gift to be able to divide our lives into different pieces, but to be whole or to have integrity means to be one seamless piece. Try not to segment your life. Be the same person in all situations.
- Don't keep secrets. A man of integrity keeps nothing hidden.
- Lean in to good men for accountability. Stay close to your band of brothers.

Personal Courage

Personal courage is the fuel required to make all the other core values come to life. Without personal courage, none of the other values are even possible. Again and again you'll be faced with seemingly insignificant choices, but each consistent, positive choice reflects your personal courage. Will you do the right thing even when no one else is looking? Will you sacrifice your own comfort for the sake of someone else? Will you live in a way that inspires your family to be better? Will you show up to serve even when you just don't want to?

To face fear, danger, or adversity and not turn away—that's personal courage. But so is facing your own indifference, your own doubt and confusion. Some of the biggest battles we'll ever fight are waged in our own minds. Controlling your thought life and believing what God says about you is often harder than standing in the face of danger.

These internal battles must be fought and won in our own hearts, without the cheers and support of others. This is where the true strength of a man is determined. Set it as a goal to up your courage game. Make a commitment to yourself to stand up against your own weakness. Think hard about the times when you take shortcuts and the areas in which you lack courage. Make it your goal to shut down weakness and take up courage. To conquer your own weakness is to be a warrior worthy of the Lord.

> Therefore, my dear brothers and sisters, stand firm. Let nothing move you. Always give yourselves fully to the work of the Lord, because you know that your labor in the Lord is not in vain. (1 Corinthians 15:58)

> Be strong and courageous. Do not be afraid or terrified because of them, for the Lord your God goes with you; he will never leave you nor forsake you. (Deuteronomy 31:6)

THE WHITE PHASE

The values learned in the red phase now become the foundation for action in the white phase. In the white phase of boot camp, soldiers begin to train and become expert in their use of weapons of warfare. They start target practice with their assault rifles and learn to use grenades, machine guns, grenade launchers, and heavy weaponry.

To be a successful soldier, you must know what weapons are available to you and how to use them. You must be well practiced and ready to face whatever may come. What are the weapons of warfare we need as fathers of children with special needs?

Conviction: Know What You Believe and Do Not Be Moved

At the core of everything you do, there is a firmly held belief or conviction that, if rightly and securely placed, can give you incredible motivation, stability, and courage. Conviction is a mighty weapon, able to destroy doubt and double-mindedness on contact. It anchors you and helps you stand against the lies of the Enemy. Many a man has been saved from trouble because he held firm to his convictions. The man who knows who he is in the Lord and what he was sent here to do is a man who will thrive in the face of adversity.

Mental Toughness: Don't Believe Everything You Think

One of the most important weapons you have is the ability to shoot down negative thoughts and exercise control over your own thinking. You don't have to accept every thought that passes through your mind. Many thoughts are neither from God nor from ourselves but are implanted by the Enemy of our souls to undermine us. Striking down negative thoughts and rejecting everything that doesn't line up with God's Word is your first line of defense. Self-pity, negativity, and self-centered thinking must be rooted out and destroyed . . . or they can destroy you. Be vigilant and don't believe everything you think.

Prayer: Before You Act, You Must Pray

Prayer is direct access to the power source. I urge you to make a priority of daily, humble conversation with God on behalf of your family. Clear every decision and concern with God before you act. You'll be amazed at what can be accomplished through prayer alone. This is one of your most powerful weapons!

The Sword: God's Word Is Your Greatest Offense and Strongest Defense

The good that comes from using Scripture to combat the Enemy is immeasurable. We see this weapon used by Jesus when he faced Satan in the wilderness and countered every temptation with Scripture (Matthew 4:1–11). Scripture can also act as a compass for our lives, giving us direction when we feel lost and uncertain. It is a rock of refuge when we need safety and reassurance. The more familiar you are with this weapon and the more practiced you become in using it, the more skillful you'll be at taking out the opposition and defending your position. The sword of God's Word is mighty to save. Get to know it well.

The Bond of Marriage: Two Are Better Than One

Your wife is one of your greatest assets. When the two of you join in unity and solidarity, you can lay waste to seemingly insurmountable challenges. When you join forces, you can take down the Enemy with relative ease. Deuteronomy 32:30 tells us that though one can slay a thousand, two can slay ten thousand. When you truly partner with your spouse to engage this life of special-needs parenting, you'll find your load lessened and your power multiplied. Nothing thwarts the work of darkness like a unified couple who share a spiritual strategy for life and a mutual faith that God is with them.

If you are facing this life as a single parent, please hear me say how proud I am of you. There is no denying that life is tougher when you bear full responsibility without a partner to support you. Single parents are some of the people in our community I most admire and pray the hardest for, and I know you are close to God's heart. In fact, Isaiah 54:5 says that our maker, God, is our husband. Now, that sounds strange in modern culture, but the message is clear: God is available to all of us as a leader and partner in life. He will walk with us and guide us every step of the way. Indeed, his deepest desire is to do life *with* us. If you are a single parent, whether a father or a mother, invite God to partner with you. Let that bond strengthen and encourage you. You are not alone!

Fraternity: Secure a Battle Buddy; Know Your Cadre and Squad

Another powerful source of encouragement and support can be the community of special-needs dads with whom you connect. It's essential for you to lock arms with at least one battle buddy—a special-needs dad who understands and will help encourage and support you. This community is as necessary as a soldier's squadron. You can't effectively fight alone. Make it a goal to meet other dads who are in the trenches and who will support you.

BLUE PHASE

The final phase of basic training focuses on live engagement in potential military scenarios. Soldiers are taught practical skills in real time, such as how to ride safely in a convoy, how to secure and defend a strategic position, and how to recover a hostage. This stage of training is where the rubber meets the road. Scenarios resembling real life are practiced so soldiers can get comfortable managing their equipment and making critical decisions.

In the next few chapters, we're going to look closely at the specific duties of a special-needs soldier and how our own real-life scenarios can play out. We'll dig into our blue-phase training there and learn more about how to engage each opportunity. We will delve into our duties as special-needs dads to protect and defend, provide, strengthen, and equip.

A Story from the Front Line

Retired Master Sergeant Rick Imel lives in Tennessee with his wife, Brenda, and their two children, Staci and Danny. This is a personal story from his life on the front line.

It was a brisk fall evening in 1996 when I once again found myself strapped into a Black Hawk helicopter on another mission. Unlike so many previous assignments, I didn't feel the rush of adrenaline when the metal bird lifted off. I didn't rehearse the upcoming mission as I had always done in the past. There were no shared head nods and knowing fist bumps. The confidence of past assignments was noticeably absent. Tonight we were not on a mission of national security. Tonight was personal, and I was scared to death. A medevac helicopter from Ireland Army Health Clinic in Fort Knox, Kentucky, was en route to Kosair Children's Hospital in Louisville, Kentucky. It carried me, the crew chief, two pilots, and the patient.

On this night the patient was my son. Born in August of the same year, Danny was suffering severe seizures. His condition was beyond what the army hospital was equipped to deal with. As we flew north to Louisville, I didn't watch the scenery below but instead bowed my head over my son and asked God to protect him. I felt lost because there was no battle drill to prepare me for dealing with a child with seizures. Thankfully, I knew enough to ask God for help. And God, in his great mercy, carried my family through this difficult journey that is all too common for families with special needs.

The army has an Exceptional Family Member Program that makes allowances based on the needs of a handicapped dependent. Our whole family has learned to make allowances. Danny's older sister had to mature quickly because of her brother. She suffered the double whammy of having a sibling with special needs and being a military brat. Early on she became her mother's grown-up little helper. My wife had to sacrifice her career because my multiple deployments kept me away. She was left to do the heavy lifting of raising young children in my absence. My burden was shouldering the guilt and tension of not being there for my family who had so many pressing needs.

In his wisdom God brought us to Cookeville, Tennessee, where we became a part of the ministry founded by Jeff and Becky Davidson. There we found community and support. There I found my band of brothers, other special-needs dads who get it. I am grateful to the military for teaching me everything I know about being a soldier, and I am indebted to my friend Jeff for helping me become a warrior of a different kind. I now fight for my family, and my heart's desire is to stand up for those who have no voice, who don't fit in, who need protection. This is a battle worth fighting for the rest of my life.

MISSION CRITICAL

- [ ] Commit to the seven core values.
- [ ] Practice using the weapons of our warfare.
- [ ] Engage your mission with intention and focus.

CHAPTER 4

Protect and Defend

My dad coached my Little League baseball team. He taught me how to drive. He coached my high school basketball team. He drove me to my dorm for my freshman year of college. When I got married, he was my best man. When my son was born, he was waiting in the hospital room to hold his new grandson. When I bought my first house, he went with me to meet the Realtor. When I left a high-paying corporate career and sold my dream home to start a special-needs ministry, he gave me his support. When I lay in a hospital bed fighting for my life earlier this year, he and my mom drove to sit beside me almost every day.

Now he drives me every week on a 160-mile trek to visit my medical team. When we stop for lunch on the way home, he always buys. Knowing I am on a special diet for my kidneys, he grills me a dozen diet-approved, specially seasoned steak burgers every couple of weeks. He stops by my office once a week just to see how I am doing. The other day I thanked him once again for driving me around, and he replied, "I have nothing else to do but take care of you."

Eleven words. All you need to know about being a dad in eleven words.

My dad has taken care of me for fifty years now. He needed only eleven words to define our relationship as father and son for the past fifty years.

"I have nothing else to do but take care of you."

FATHER BEGETS FATHER

I have often said that I wasn't ready to be the father of a child with special needs.

I have written about being unprepared, ill-equipped, and clueless about how to be a dad to a child with special needs. I realize now that I knew more than I thought.

I knew what really mattered most because my dad had demonstrated it to me.

I knew how to embrace a son with unconditional love.

I knew how to be involved and engaged.

I knew that my primary job was to take care of my son.

Quite simply, I knew how to "be there."

I know these things because I was taught by a good man, a man who made me his priority—in sickness and in health. I owe him a debt of gratitude for all he has done for me and am thankful for such a powerful example of selfless love.

I'm one of the lucky ones. But what if you didn't have a good dad? What if you were emotionally neglected or your dad wasn't there at all? What if your dad was an alcoholic or an addict? What if he just didn't make time for you? It's essential to your success as a dad to look at the example that was set for you. If you didn't have a strong father, you're going to feel less equipped to handle fatherhood. You may even unintentionally bring some unhealthy baggage to your current family dynamic.

In the upcoming chapters, I want you to consider the impact your father had on how you think about protecting and defending your family, providing for them, strengthening them, and equipping them. Do your own risk assessment based on what you've been given to work with. This isn't about judging your father's lack or your own; it's about knowing yourself. Try to determine whether you're at risk in any of these areas, and if so, let me encourage you with this: no matter what kind of father you had, your heavenly Father is ready and willing to fill in any gaps you may have missed. He'll instruct you in a highly personal way if you'll just ask him. Invite his help. Ask for wisdom. Ask for healing.

THE WATCHMAN

While you may not have to face grenades or rocket launchers as a special-needs dad, there will be plenty of times when you'll confront real threats and danger. Some of you have children who have multiple seizures every day; others must cope with the constant fear of a medical crisis or even the death of your child. Many of you have children who are prone to public outbursts that make life unpredictable and stressful. You face judgmental outsiders, indifferent service providers, less-than-competent medical staff, and a school system ill-equipped to help. You live with the threat of financial ruin or the knowledge that you can't provide all your family needs. Often resources you desperately need are not available. It takes a well-trained soldier to protect and defend his family against the onslaught of attacks against them. This life isn't easy, and our families are often overwhelmed.

So what does it mean to protect and defend your family? How do you do it?

A special-needs father is the first line of defense for his family, the filter through which everything must pass. He's the rock on whom his family can lean. He stands in the watchtower and keeps vigilant surveillance, on continuous alert for anything that might pose a threat to his family. He listens carefully to God for instructions and leads his family well. He's their guardian, their champion, their watchdog. He protects them—body, soul, and spirit.

Did you know that every human being is made up of three parts? We consist of a body, a soul (your mind, will, and emotions), and a spirit. This truth is found in 1 Thessalonians 5:23: "May God himself, the God of peace, sanctify you through and through. May your whole spirit, soul and body be kept blameless at the coming of our Lord Jesus Christ." Even though my son is nonverbal and can seem mentally and emotionally disconnected, he isn't. Neither is yours. We each have a body, soul, and spirit that need protection and support—especially children who are mentally and physically impaired. Without question, they need the most protection because they're utterly unable to protect themselves.

Let me speak specifically to those of you who have a profoundly impaired child, as I do. Don't be deceived: just because your child can't speak or respond like a typical child doesn't mean he or she isn't in need of tenderness, protection, and connection. Your son is aware in his *spirit* even if not in his mind. Your daughter is aware of the mood of people around her, of the attitudes and actions of the people who care for her, even though she can't acknowledge this.

Jill Bolte Taylor, a brain scientist at Harvard, suffered a stroke in 1996 that wiped out the left hemisphere of her brain. Fortunately, she made a full recovery that allowed her to share what she had learned from her experience. After the stroke, Jill woke up with no awareness of her past, her identity, her prior knowledge, or her language. She was left with one thing: she was present. She didn't recognize her family or friends, but she reports that she could tell who was "for her" and who wasn't. She was intensely aware of the motivations of people. Her mother came to see her at the hospital, and she recalls that she was overwhelmingly aware that this woman, whoever she was, was "for her" even though she didn't recognize her.

When someone seems as though they're mentally "missing," *you have to go in and find them.*

Her ordeal taught her many things, but I want to share two specific details. First, she said she wanted people to know that when someone seems as though they're mentally "missing," *you have to go in and find them*. That's what happened when I made funny noises for Jon Alex. I "found him" inside his world. She also said that when people don't experience the typical mental distractions of life, they're much more keenly aware of the energy everyone brings into the room. She urges us to take responsibility for the energy or attitude we bring to any situation, most of all toward impaired people, because they're most sensitive to it. Just because your child is mentally "missing" doesn't mean he or she isn't "there." All our children need love and protection on every level.[7]

It's probably easiest to grasp what it means to protect your child's physical body. You watch out for him, making sure he's safe and out of harm's way. You stand between her and physical threats. You protect his health by guiding his choices in food, clothing, and safety. You oversee her physical well-being by watching carefully and being aware of her needs—hunger, thirst, and the alleviation of pain. As your child's shield, you do all you can to stay strong by caring for your own physical health and well-being.

As for protection of the soul, that's a little less obvious, but I know you can think of ways you can help safeguard the mind, will, and emotions of each family member. You openly show each of them they're loved and cared for. You guide their media exposure, avoiding what will frighten, overwhelm, or harm them. You encourage them to express their emotional needs, and you provide comfort and support by being a good listener and caring about what they say. A father is the safe refuge where people come to talk when they have a problem, the stabilizing force that keeps everyone together. But to be this kind of father, you must take care of your own soul. You must pay close attention to what you watch, listen to, and think about.

The spirit of your child and your family is also in need of protection. The Enemy will often try to overwhelm us with discouragement, fear, and anger. We can get so down in our spirit that we're tempted to give in to despair. Our spirits need to be fed by God. You can encourage this by praying daily—sometimes many times a day—for the protection and deliverance of your family from anything or anyone that might threaten to harm their spirit. You can encourage your family's involvement in church, read Scriptures and stories to them, and even recount your own experiences of God's faithfulness. Doing these things requires that you take good care of your own spirit by immersing yourself in God's Word and prayer. By doing this you build a hedge of protection around your family that will help keep them safe.

All three areas—the body, the soul, and the spirit—need protection from threats both visible and invisible. This requires great leadership and a willingness to seek God often for help. You may not realize your family is under spiritual attack unless you're regularly praying and listening for God's voice. Nor will you know your children are in physical or emotional danger unless you're involved and engaged in their lives.

The Lord is your defender and protector, and he'll teach you to fill the same role for your family.

You must be a brave soldier, trusting in your commanding officer, the Creator of the universe, both to have your back and to forge the way ahead of you. You must be involved and present every day. If you get tired, lazy, or complacent and look away, the Enemy can take advantage of you, so it's imperative always to remain vigilant. The job of protector and defender can seem overwhelming unless you bear ever in mind who it is you work for and how infinitely powerful he is. The Lord is your defender and protector, and he'll teach you to fill the same role for your family.

Let me give you a real-life example of how God protects us when we listen and obey. As I have told you, in my early years I was a successful salesman. Becky and I had a comfortable life and lacked for nothing. I was living the American dream, but God was drawing my heart toward service. Becky and I had recently launched Rising Above, a ministry designed to encourage and equip families who have children with special needs. We were hosting monthly church services and small events. We loved it, but being an insurance salesman was my security and my identity. It was who I was.

Around that same time, my pastor, a dear friend and someone I truly respect, started asking me to go to lunch . . . often. Naturally, I became curious. What was he up to? What did he want? Maybe he needed a donation and was building up the courage to ask me.

Maybe he wanted advice on life insurance. I wasn't at all sure of his agenda, but I was in no way prepared for what he finally revealed.

One day as we sat down together, he began to share his heart. It seemed he thought I would make a good addition to the pastoral staff at church. *Wait—what?* I thought to myself. I mean, come on—I'm no pastor—and besides, that would mean like an 80 percent decrease in income. I mean, *seriously*? This couldn't be real, but I agreed to "think about it."

You may already know this, but when the Lord initiates something in you, you never know where it might take you. I sincerely wanted to obey God's leading, but this was just over the top! I was a businessman—and a good one at that. Little by little the tug grew stronger, and after much prayer and many conversations with my wife, I said yes. This was, I knew full well, career suicide. I was walking away from everything I had built and every success-centered goal I cared about. We would have to sell our home, give up my beloved swimming pool, and move farther out of town. My parents and friends would surely think we had lost it—and maybe we had—but we felt compelled to obey.

The transition was made, and my new life as a staff pastor began. It seemed an insane choice to have made—maybe even reckless, but we believed it was right. Little by little I became less businessman and more brother. I loved the staff, enjoyed hanging out with godly men, and loved serving. It was a different world than the one I had left: less cutthroat, more kind, less striving, more peace, less financial security, more faith. I had obeyed, and God was taking care of us, but I had no idea at the time how much.

About a year after I started working for the church, I had a medical crisis that put me in the hospital. It was a critical health event that was going to completely change my life. I couldn't work—or do much of anything else. My church family was my rock. The elders prayed for me. They pulled money out of their own pockets and handed it to me. They encouraged me and stood by us in selfless service. I felt covered, loved, and supported, and my family was taken care of.

It didn't take long to realize an incredible truth: if I hadn't obeyed God and gone to work for the church, I would have been not only critically ill, but also unemployed. There is no doubt in my mind that my corporate position would have been terminated for failure to perform. My illness persists, and so has the love of my church. I have been supported and held up by their steadfast love for years now. What would have become of us if I had still been a corporate cog? I hate to think.

The upshot of this story is straightforward: if you listen and obey, your loving Father will direct and protect you. The best thing I did to protect my family was to be there in the center of God's will for my life, even though what he asked me to do appeared both utterly foolish and financially irresponsible. Gentlemen, the best way to protect your family is to follow the orders of your Commander in Chief.

PROTECT YOUR NEST

Another way I practice the duty to protect and defend is to keep a close watch on other people's drama. Everyone has problems, and we all need support from time to time, but there are people who seem to thrive on drama. In the Davidson household we have a "Protect the Nest" policy, and it has been critical to our success. I keep a close watch on anything that tries to upset the delicate balance of our family life, and any influx of outside drama is strictly prohibited. As is inside drama. We work hard to keep ourselves in check and to maintain the peace of our household. It's essential.

I cannot overestimate the importance of the no-drama policy. Our special-needs families are already stressed far beyond the norm, so we can't afford to allow unnecessary chaos in our homes—even from within our own extended families. Men, determine to be the gatekeeper of what comes into your home. If someone outside is creating drama, shut it down. If your own people are disturbing the peace of the household, speak directly to the issue. It's okay to say, "You aren't permitted to disturb the peace of this house!" That peace must remain sacred and inviolate.

In all fairness, this can be tricky with kids who have frequent meltdowns. I encourage you to use your best judgment and determine with your spouse what are fair expectations for your family. The point is to keep a watch over the peace of your home and teach your family the importance of this principle. Teach them to love peace. Drama is more destructive than it may seem, and we need to limit it as much as possible. Remember that if you grew up with a lot of drama, you may be prone to it yourself, so consider that as well.

Think for a moment about how your dad protected and defended you. Did you feel safe? Did you feel as though you could have gone to him with your fears or concerns? If you didn't have a good protector for a dad, ask God to show you what one looks like. Press in to your band of brothers for advice and support. Dig into a Bible study, such as *Stepping Up: A Call to Courageous Manhood* by Dennis Rainey. It is a strong study on manhood that I have used and benefited from. You can't do better than your example unless you make up your mind to reach higher than the bar that was set for you.

To be the guardian of your family is a tremendous responsibility. I want to help you understand what that means. I also want to give you as many tools as I can to help you succeed. I want to introduce a system that has helped many soldiers and civilians create successful plans of action for specific challenges. This system was developed by the military, and I believe it can help you in several ways.

SMEAC

SMEAC (pronounced "smee·ack") is an acronym for *s*ituation, *m*ission, *e*xecution, *a*dministration, and *c*ommand. Using this system to plan strategies for your family can be very useful. It can help you be a proactive father, improve communication within your family, and keep you and your spouse on the same page, preempting problems by planning ahead.

The SMEAC strategy system is designed to transfer critical details about a mission to the troops in a clear and concise manner. It is an excellent way to communicate goals and objectives and how they should be achieved. It is successfully used by the military and has been adopted by businesses, nonprofits, and individuals as well. We are going to employ it to illustrate the breakdown of a specific duty and how to successfully accomplish it. Following is the explanation for each aspect.

Situation

This is where you report the background and specifics of your focused mission: the what, when, where, and why of things. The point is to set up the backdrop for the instructions that will follow.

Mission

The mission outlines the planned response to the situation or problem described above. This should be a short, clear, and concise statement. The details will follow.

Execution

This is the "how" part of the SMEAC. Here you provide specific details as to how you will accomplish your mission. This section is longer and provides explicit instruction.

Administration

Here you detail what resources will be needed to complete the mission and how those resources will be coordinated.

Command

This is the who's who of the job—who's in charge, who you report to, and how you communicate with each other.

Let's use this system to break down a protect-and-defend moment for your family so you'll have a practical example of how this works. I'll apologize in advance for the fact that there's no way to represent the wide variety of needs that fall into the category of "special needs." Some of these examples won't correlate with your family situation at all, though hopefully others will. Our children fall on vastly different points along the continuum of need. All of them matter. All of them are important. If your situation isn't represented, don't think for one second that it isn't valid. The SMEAC is a tool to empower you. The point of using it is to help you take a proactive role in your family. It's a leadership tool. I urge you to adopt the model and apply it to your family.

Almost every special-needs family with a child attending public school will face IEP meetings. IEP stands for Individualized Education Program. These meetings are designed to discuss your child's educational needs and goals. You'll meet with your child's team to discuss their present level of performance (PLOP), annual goals, and individualized supports and services.

IEP meetings are often stressful and upsetting for families. Most of the stress comes from the pressure parents feel to advocate for their child and secure the services they believe are needed and warranted. The other tough thing about IEP meetings is the focus put on scales and measures that point to how impaired your child is. No matter how aware you are of your child's deficits, it's painful to have them pointed out so openly in public. Many times, IEP meetings are left for moms to deal with, but that isn't always the best protect-and-defend posture for the family. I have always been a part of these meetings, but it's important for you to determine together what's best for your family. A little preparation and focus before the meeting can help protect your family on many levels.

Let's apply SMEAC and create a plan that protects and defends your family. I'll use our family as an example. This is a very formal outline for the sake of explanation. You can make the process quick and painless if you use the SMEAC format with your own shorthand.

Situation

An IEP meeting for Jon Alex has been scheduled for next week. He needs more help with nonverbal communication tools in the classroom. He also needs better supervision at mealtimes because he hasn't been eating well. Typically, we leave these meetings feeling discouraged. We need a fresh plan to communicate his needs and stay positive about his progress.

Mission

We will attend Jon Alex's IEP meeting and successfully advocate for his needs, while protecting our family's dignity.

Execution

- Both of us will attend the IEP meeting because it is too much stress to put on one parent alone.
- We will pray together before we go into the meeting and put on our spiritual armor (Ephesians 6:10–18).
- We will begin our portion by thanking the staff for their support, detailing specific things for which we're grateful.
- We will ask for an evaluation of possible nonverbal tools that could assist with his communication.
- We will ask for better supervision at mealtimes.
- We will talk about our satisfaction that, even though he scores below the curve in many areas, he is kind and gentle. We will share the positives we see about him.
- We will walk away with a strong plan in place and remember that Jon Alex's weaknesses can't begin to compare with his worth and value as an agent of change in this world.

Administration

- Take separate cars so that Jeff can return to work.
- Bring our individual lists and the family IEP notebook.
- Do research on any new, simplified Proloquo2Go tools that might help Jon Alex communicate.

Command

- Pray before meeting—Jeff
- List of specific things we are grateful to the staff for—Becky
- List of concerns—Jeff
- Debrief after meeting—Both

SMEAC is a simple way to attack problems and distribute labor. It sends a message to your family and to the public that you're a dad who's involved and on top of things. It's also a tool that helps you protect and defend your family. Keep it simple, and it will serve you well.

To protect and defend your family will require all the resources you have at your disposal. You will need to stay alert and be aware of all that is happening in your home and with each member of your family. Remember that they need your protection on three levels: body, soul, and spirit. One of the most helpful ways you can protect your family is to remain in the center of God's will for your life. And don't forget to keep drama at a minimum and "protect your nest."

Encouragement from the Homefront . . .
A Letter from Becky

Brave Soldier,

Thank you for your faithful service to your wife and family. You're far more important to them than you may realize. You have been commissioned by God to love, protect, and defend your family. To carry out this mission, you'll have to learn to rely on God's guidance. You weren't meant to do this alone.

One of the things I appreciated most about Jeff was knowing that I could come to him with my concerns and fears. He was my refuge, my best friend and confidante. There were nights when I would wake up, battered by fear or worried and unable to sleep. I knew that I could wake him and share my concerns. I never worried that he would be angry or frustrated with me.

He would hold me, pray for me, and take authority as the leader of our household over whatever was troubling me. After he would pray, I could go back to sleep in peace, assured that I was safe. Jeff was the spiritual leader of our home, and he knew that God was the true source of our protection. Because of his trust in God, I could trust Jeff to make the best decisions for our family.

Soldier, you have what it takes to be the leader, protector, husband,

and father God wants you to be. Rise up and be the man your family needs. I believe in you.

Blessings from the Homefront,
Becky

MISSION CRITICAL

- ☐ Determine to protect and defend your family.
- ☐ Ask God for guidance and help in doing this.
- ☐ Use the tools provided in this chapter to diligently guard your people.

CHAPTER 5

Provide

The American psyche is deeply rooted in rugged individualism. This belief system asserts that people should succeed on their own, without the intervention of others. The idea is wonderful in theory but fatally flawed and in no way biblical. The "pull yourself up by your own bootstraps" philosophy places sole responsibility on the individual for success. This would be great if we never aged or had any health issues, if we were always at our best and never lacked for inspiration or inventiveness.

The truth is that we were created to be interdependent brothers (like soldiers in a regiment) who are completely dependent upon the goodness of God as our source. Anything else is doomed to fail. Ask yourself honestly: What is my source? Is it your job, your own strength, your investment portfolio, or your quick wit and irresistible charm?

For men, it's easy to feel as though we're in charge of our own destiny. I felt that way for years. I was confident and secure in my own ability and felt as though I didn't really have to lean on God for much of anything. In a moment, all of that changed. An unexpected health crisis left me dependent on everyone around me. I found out quickly that depending on myself as my "source" was foolhardy. The years that have followed have consisted of one medical crisis after another, and with each one my awareness of my own lack and God's willingness to provide has increased.

The first rule of being a provider is that you're only as good as your source. A soldier going into battle can be professionally trained and fully prepared, but he's only as good as his equipment and source of provision. Without the proper tools and a steady supply line, he can't do his job. So it is for us. The question we must settle, then, is this: What is our source?

In reality, none of us is "enough" in and of ourselves to provide for our families in the way they truly need and deserve. To give them what they need—body, soul, and spirit—requires the knowledge, guidance, and provision of God. The good thing is that we have his word that he will be our true source if we are only willing to trust and follow him. Listen to these promises from Scripture. Let them sink deeply into your mind and heart. As long as we put our faith in him, our one true source is inexhaustible and ever present.

> The lions may grow weak and hungry, but those who seek the LORD lack no good thing. (Psalm 34:10)

> So do not worry, saying, "What shall we eat?" or "What shall we drink?" or "What shall we wear?" For the pagans run after all these things, and your heavenly Father knows that you need them. (Matthew 6:31–32)

> He who did not spare his own Son, but gave him up for us all—how will he not also, along with him, graciously give us all things? (Romans 8:32)

Be assured that God will help you provide for your family in every way if you will only put your trust in him. Don't wait until a crisis to make this decision. Give your full heart to him and ask him to show you how to be a good provider.

God will not only provide for you, but in the same self-sacrificing way that he gave up his Son, he will teach you to give sacrificially to your family. All you need to do is be willing and ask for help. This level of commitment is costly, but it is also where true peace, purpose, and meaning are found.

IT'S NOT WHAT YOU SAY, IT'S WHAT YOU DO

A soldier's life has a great deal to do with physical and mental discipline, but *being* a soldier is so much more than that—it is a way of life. A lot of men think that parenting is just about discipline, as though controlling how a child acts will make them a good person. Of course, discipline is important, and it has a very necessary place, but it isn't enough. The truth is that Jesus came to bring salvation and to teach us *how to live*. He didn't go around correcting everyone's behavior all the time. He lived his life loving and serving others so that we could see what God and godly living really look like.

In John 14:9, Jesus says, "Anyone who has seen me has seen the Father." Charles Finney (1792–1875), a well-known American minister and leader in the Second Great Awakening, commented on Acts 10:38, which tells us that Jesus "went around doing good." Finney said, "Jesus Christ went about promoting the well-being of men wherever he went. . . . It is implied that this was his business—the thing he had above all things else at heart. For this end he came into the world. He came to do good and not evil; to bless and not to curse; to fill the world with peace, love and happiness, so far as lay within the range of his influence. The good of man was the great object which he sought."[8] Jesus is our example, so I ask you, what is your "business"? What is the thing you have above all else in your heart?

Your example is the first and arguably the most important resource you provide your children.

I ask this question because yours is the example your children will follow. Your example is the first and arguably the most important resource you provide your children. What you teach them will be supported or undermined by the example you set. If a staff sergeant orders his men to be ready for drills at a certain hour and then fails to show up, he immediately compromises the respect he has developed with his men. So it is with parenting. It's never just what you say but always what you *do* that matters. It's your example that your children and spouse will remember long after you're gone.

My father showed me I was important to him by including me and being deeply involved in my life. I never wondered whether he cared. I never had to. What kind of example did your dad set? What kind of a provider was he? Keep that question in mind as we move through this chapter. Ask yourself how you want to be remembered by your children.

American culture has become so focused on material things that when we think of providing for our family, it's hard for us to think beyond financial provision. In truth, financial provision is in many ways less important than the other ways in which we need to provide. As fathers, we need to remember that we're trying to build happy, wholehearted adults. We inherently know that providing for our children's emotional needs is more important than providing them with the newest and best "stuff," but following through on that conviction can be a tougher job. Too often we find it easier to provide for our families financially than to give our whole selves to serve them. Let's look at some of the ways we need to provide that don't involve money.

Consistency

One of the best and most effective ways in which we can meet the needs of our family is to simply be consistent. Easier said than done, I know, but it makes such a difference for your family to know that you can be depended upon to act and respond in a predictable way, no matter what. If your children disobey, they know you will hold them accountable. If they need support, they know you will be there. If consistency is a struggle for you, ask God to reveal the root of the problem. Anger can often upset that balance, as can apathy. Both of these feelings can suggest a heart problem that needs to be dealt with.

A Place to Vent and Get Advice

Dads provide an important service to their families when they let them vent their feelings without judging or shutting them down. We can also be a great source of advice and support, but we must prove ourselves trustworthy. No one wants to talk to someone they can't trust. Be the person your kids can come to for talking things out. Be a good listener.

Opportunity/Permission to Fail

Perfect behavior shouldn't be our goal for our kids. Children need to learn from us *how to live*. That means that we provide many opportunities for them to try and fail. Whenever they fall short, we provide loving support and new ideas for how to succeed on the next attempt. Childhood is the time to try, fail, and learn. Dads can provide a safe place for that to happen.

Leadership

One of the most important assets a father supplies is leadership. A family needs a strong, decisive leader—and you can be that leader. There's great safety in knowing that your dad is at the helm and that he has plotted a course for the family. We must lead our families safely and securely into the future. If you don't feel confident about your leadership skills, seek out a father you admire and talk to him. Asking for help is wise and shows strength.

Hope and Inspiration

Dads set the tone for the family in many ways. We can crush our people if we don't show them respect, and we can also be a source of inspiration and hope. The special-needs life is fraught with setbacks and disappointments. Determine to be a dad who raises the hope of the team. Be the one who cheers everyone on and calls them up. Lift your family with your heart of hope and love for them.

Fun

One of the greatest ways a dad can connect is to be fun. We are the ones who wrestle, tickle, and roughhouse, and our families need that release. If this isn't your style, then find another way to play. Create an atmosphere of cheer, and you'll have lifelong followers.

The Definition of a Man

Your example will be the single most important influence on what your children expect men to be. That's a huge responsibility. Your little girl will either look for a man like you or seek one who's totally different. Your son will emulate you . . . or rebel against you. Take a serious look at what you're conveying to your family about who men are. This alone will determine much about what kind of people they become.

Spiritual Guidance

As a father you have the great privilege of leading your family closer to God. This requires that you let your own heart be drawn closer to him. The best thing you can do for your family is to fall more deeply in love with Christ. Out of this love you will naturally guide them into a deeper spiritual walk.

Always remember that you're providing for the physical (body), emotional (soul), and spiritual (spirit) needs of your family. There are hundreds of ways in which fathers provide, but these are some important ones.

Finally, we'll touch on the financial responsibility we carry as fathers.

MONEY MATTERS—BUT NOT AS MUCH AS YOU MIGHT THINK

I recently read an article suggesting that some of the very best fathers aren't the most financially successful. I can certainly see how that could be the case. When I was busy making money, I had little time to devote to my family. Jon Alex had every toy he could possibly have wanted, but he didn't have me. It's our duty and responsibility to provide for our family financially. In fact, Scripture has some surprisingly strong words to say about this: "Anyone who does not provide for their relatives, and especially for their own household, has denied the faith and is worse than an unbeliever" (1 Timothy 5:8).

So how do we do this in a way that honors God?

I want to tell you a story about an incredible man of faith. His name was George Müller.

Müller was born in Prussia, now Germany, in 1805. In his early years he was a rebellious troublemaker. By the age of ten, he was described as a thief, a liar, and a gambler. In 1825, he attended a prayer meeting, where his transformation began. He heard the gospel preached and felt convicted in his heart. Soon he became a Christian and immediately stopped drinking, stealing, lying, and gambling. His father wanted him to become a clergyman—a position of influence and honor, but Müller felt compelled to become a missionary instead.[9]

Müller began preaching and eventually moved to England. He was a firm believer in prayer and in the willingness of God to provide for our every need. He was eventually led to establish the Ashley Down Orphanage in Bristol, England. In his lifetime he cared for more than 10,000 orphans and established 117 schools that offered Christian education to 120,000 children, many of whom were also orphans. He also founded the Scriptural Knowledge Institution and was responsible for distributing hundreds of thousands of Bibles, New Testaments, and other biblical materials during his lifetime.[10]

The thought of providing for thousands of children is staggering, but the most remarkable thing was that he never asked for one dime. Instead, he prayed continuously that the Lord would move the hearts of men and women to give. God brought millions of dollars in gifts over his lifetime, which he directed to these works without ever once soliciting funds.

Müller's faith in God's willingness to provide is still an inspiration today. One of my favorite stories is about a time when the orphanage ran out of food. All the children were assembled for breakfast, but there was nothing to feed them. George instructed them to sit down together, pray, and wait. If this had been me, I would have been freaking out—but not George. They waited quietly in faith, and soon a knock came at the door. The baker was there, and he reported that the Lord had woken him in the night and instructed him to bake bread for the children. He delivered enough bread to feed them all. Just after that the milkman arrived at the door. His cart had broken down in front of the orphanage, and he offered them all his milk. God had provided in the nick of time, and Müller never had to ask a single soul for anything.[11]

**God is the real provider—
the one true source.**

This kind of faith inspires me and reminds me that God is the real provider—the one true source. George developed his incredible faith over time. He was devoted to prayer and grew in his ability to discern God's will, but, like me, he conceded that he would often have to work very hard to settle his mind so he could hear from God. He reported that he would put his finger on a promise in the Bible and then pray that promise until he was settled and focused in his heart. He also wrote about his process for making a prayerful decision. Pay close attention to his steps:

1. Before entering into prayer, he would wait till his heart was at a place where it *had no will of its own*. Müller felt that nine-tenths of the problem most people experience in this regard is allowing their own agenda to cloud their ability to hear God clearly.
2. Next, he would pray and discern, though he wouldn't depend on his impression alone.
3. He would seek the Lord both in prayer and in the Word. He realized that his impression of what God was saying had to line up with Scripture for him to accept it as true.
4. Next, he considered providential circumstances. What did

God seem to be doing? This would often point him in the right direction.

5. He then asked God to clearly reveal his will.
6. Finally, through prayer, study, and reflection, he would come to a deliberate decision. If he remained at peace about the decision after a few more times of prayer, he would move forward.[12]

This is an incredible example of patiently waiting for God to lead and provide. It's an example we aren't likely to consider in this fast-paced world of instant gratification, but if we really want to walk with God, we must be willing to spend time with him and wait for his direction for next steps. This method clearly worked for George, it has worked for me, and I believe it will work for you too.

REALITY CHECK

What happens if you have sought the Lord and are honestly doing all you know how to do to provide for your family, but you still can't afford something your child really needs? I know men who have been crushed by the pain of being unable to provide an expensive piece of equipment or a necessary service because of limited financial resources. This is a very real scenario in the lives of special-needs families. Almost all of us face it to one degree or another. As the providers and leaders of our families, it's easy for us to feel shame and diminishment when we can't find a way to access what our children need. It can kill our confidence and shut us down. What should we do?

I believe that in situations such as this, it's important to remember that God calls us to be the body of Christ. First Corinthians 12:25–27 says, "There should be no division in the body, but that its parts should have equal concern for each other. If one part suffers, every part suffers with it; if one part is honored, every part rejoices with it. Now you are the body of Christ, and each one of you is a part of it."

We have lived for decades as a society of independent, "self-made" people. We are individuals struggling side by side, but seldom do we come to each other's aid. We make our own way and don't often think of the needs of those around us. Our pride has grown to a staggering level, and we don't know, as communities once did, how to share our burdens.

Long ago people came together to build barns, clear land, and dig wells because they knew that each of these tasks was too big for any one man to accomplish. I think there are times when we are meant to reach out for help. I believe God honors the prayer of absolute faith *and* the beauty of community. The important thing is to ask him and follow his lead.

I'VE FALLEN . . .

I used to roll my eyes every time the "I've fallen and I can't get up" commercial came on TV. My friends and I made a joke of it and worked it into our humor routine. Then, one afternoon, that very thing happened to me. I was recovering from extensive surgery on both my feet and was in a wheelchair with casts on my legs. My legs had become very weak because of inactivity. It's amazing how quickly you "lose it if you don't use it." I was having to learn to walk all over again. One afternoon I decided to go out onto the screened-in porch to enjoy the sunshine and fresh air. I was proudly showing off my ability to walk with just a cane when it happened.

Just so you know, pride not only goes *before* a fall but it goes with you all the way down! My cane tip got caught on the rug. It went one way, and I went another. In one swift move, I hit the ground. Now what? I certainly didn't have the muscle strength to get up on my own, my wife couldn't lift me, our neighbors were at work . . .

I was channeling that commercial as I sat on the floor pondering my options. I really had fallen, and I really and truly couldn't get up. We tried everything we could think of, but it just wasn't happening. Swallowing the last shred of my dignity, I called the nonemergency number of our local emergency services. I was so humiliated I considered using a fake name when they answered. I explained my situation to the dispatcher, who could not have been more kind or understanding as he assured me that someone would be right over to help. Just a few minutes later, a two-man crew arrived. In no time they had me off the floor and safely in a chair. They were incredibly kind and helpful. They reminded me that, day or night, they were there if I needed them. All I had to do was call.

For us as special-needs fathers, there are days when we feel overwhelmed. The stress, the responsibilities, and the ongoing decision-making and action required of us can leave us feeling as though we've fallen and can't get back up. Yet all too often we don't ask for help.

The reality is that we must be willing to let others help us when we are in need. We cannot be afraid to ask for help from a friend, a family member, or someone from our church. If we forgo their help, we are robbing them of the opportunity to be a blessing. We can't simply isolate ourselves. We need each other, and we must be brave and let other people into our lives. Our willingness to be vulnerable might be the very thing that allows them to ask for help when they feel desperate and alone.

Everyone falls from time to time. Don't be afraid to ask for help. Sometimes simply admitting that you need help is the most courageous thing you can do. If it's financial help you need, ask God to lead you. Open your heart to possibilities. There may be a creative way to raise funds for a big purchase or exchange services for an item you need. Our special families need to organize to share what we have and help each other along.

As an exercise to make this a little more tangible, let's SMEAC a situation in which you might need to provide for your family. Birthday parties are often a challenge, so let's see what that might look like for you as a provider. We will use a pretend situation to demonstrate, but hopefully it's one you can identify with on some level.

Situation

Next month is Amber's birthday, and big events are always stressful for our family because our other kids don't always want to go along with her ideas. Amber, who is wheelchair bound, desperately wants to have a princess party in a castle where everyone comes in costume. This isn't easily achievable on our current budget, so we'll have to improvise. She also wants me to dress up as a prince . . . an idea which I must admit I do not look forward to.

Mission

Provide Amber with an unforgettable birthday party that is budget friendly, fun, and as stress-free as possible.

Execution

- Secure four refrigerator boxes from the appliance store.
- Clear the garage and paint the boxes bright pink with gray stonework.
- Cut large passages in two of the boxes so that Amber's wheelchair can pass through.
- Place smaller boxes on top that are also painted pink.
- Arrange the boxes in a large square and connect with ribbon.
- Draw a stone walkway leading to the castle on the driveway with chalk.
- Assign each of our others kids a role for the party: jester, maid, footman, and cook.
- Secure costumes from the thrift store (including tights, a long jacket, and a crown for "the prince").
- Prepare pink princess treats and gift bags.
- Plan games and activities, keeping our guests with special needs specifically in mind.
- Arrange for princess music, a CD player, and an outside power source.
- Pray daily for the party to deeply bless Amber, her friends, and our family.

Administration

- Dad will try to maintain a positive attitude about all the pink princess stuff and about having to dress up himself. Lead by example!

- Dad will secure boxes, borrow a truck, pick up boxes, and get them painted. Do full castle installation before the weekend of the party.
- Dad will coordinate the kids to help paint and prepare.
- Family will go together to the thrift store to secure costumes for everyone.
- Mom will plan and prepare food and gift bags, with help from the kids.
- Family will have a planning night to discuss games and plan activities.
- Amber will pick the music she wants, and Dad will make sure the system works.
- Guest list will be divided among family members, and we will each pray for our assigned guests for a week before the party. (Dad will remind family that everything we do is an outreach through which the love of Jesus can be shown.)

Command (Day of Party)

- Mom is the chief coordinator for the day. She oversees the schedule and timing of events.
- Dad oversees set up of the event, making sure the castle and everything else is ready and in place.
- Family will be in full costume and ready for event by 10:45 a.m.
- Dad will oversee greeting guests (in costume) with Amber.
- Mom will coordinate all food, games, and gifts.
- Family will make celebrating Amber their chief focus on this day.

I have never had to throw a princess party, but we've had some fun celebrations for Jon Alex. In this scenario the father is providing leadership, hope, inspiration, and fun. He is also teaching his kids what a man does. He rolls up his sleeves and gets involved, even if that means becoming a pink-princess-party prince. Love provides what the heart needs.

Encouragement from the Homefront . . . A Letter from Becky

Brave Soldier,

Thank you for the many ways in which you provide for your family. Your role as provider is a reflection of God to your family. Your wife and children learn a lot about who God is by how you provide for them–notice that I didn't say what you provide but how. Here's what I mean: If a father is joyful and generous, his children will see God as joyful and generous. If he is selfish and withholding, they will see God that way too. Always bear in mind that you are sculpting how your children see God by how you live.

When Jeff was younger, he was all about business. It was his focus and passion. Jon Alex and I had everything we desired and more, but we didn't have Jeff, and that was all we wanted. Your family wants you, not what you can provide for them materially. If finances are tough, remember that there are so many things that can make your family happy, like playing games or spending time with you. You don't have to make a lot of money to be a success as a father.

One of the things I most appreciated about Jeff was that he made me feel safe. He provided us with a feeling of ease and security. I never felt as though I had to walk on eggshells around him. He was quick with a joke and a smile. He loved to tell one-liners and sing classic '80s hits. There was always laughter in our home. You can provide so much joy for your family just by being open and available to them.

I love this quote by Maya Angelou: "I've learned that people will forget what you said, people will forget what you did, but people will never forget how you made them feel." I encourage you, brave soldiers, to think about how you make your family feel. That is what they will remember about you. Make it count. You've got this!

Blessings from the Homefront,
Becky

MISSION CRITICAL

- [ ] Acknowledge your one true source.
- [ ] Set your mind to provide for your family, not only financially but in all the ways they need.
- [ ] Don't be afraid to ask when you need help. This is bravery.

CHAPTER 6

Strengthen

To strengthen something is to fortify it, to make it stronger. In the military it's critical that each man and woman be as fit and strong as possible so they can help advance the mission. So it is with us. Special-needs families must be strong to survive. We must function as a team, share the burdens, and remain close to make it through the daily battles we face. The Enemy uses every difficult situation in life to try to tear us apart. That's why we see the failure of so many marriages after a diagnosis of special needs. There are many men who simply aren't strong enough or secure enough in themselves to stay committed. The stress and strain of our lives isn't "typical," and so our approach to life can't be typical either. We must try harder and have better strategies for overcoming.

HOW TO FORTIFY A SPECIAL-NEEDS FAMILY

Throughout history, armies have attempted to fortify cities and dwellings by building thick walls and barriers to ward off attack. This outward fortification is necessary and can be critical to success. Outward fortification of your family looks much like my earlier example of "protecting the nest," whereby we deliberately and intentionally keep drama out of our lives. It can also involve defending our homes with prayer, which creates a strong hedge of safety around us. In this chapter we want to turn our focus to internal fortification. Strengthening the inner core of our family affords us the best chance of survival. If a father is a willing guide for his family in these ways, he'll see them growing stronger and healthier. Let's look at ways we can strengthen the core of our families and not just survive but thrive.

Practice Self-Care

This may seem like a strange place to start, but self-care is foundational to maintaining a healthy family. Dads, your job is to see that everyone, including yourself, is making time to be restored and replenished. It's part of your job to make sure your wife is getting breaks. Rotate between the two of you, taking turns doing whatever it is that rests and restores you. It's vitally important to know what specific activities are life-giving for you and to be intentional about doing them. You may think that television and social media are restorative, but the reality is that most of the time they aren't.

Challenge yourself to try new things. Give a new hobby a go or pick a new trail to hike. Invite a friend to join you. Do not neglect time in nature, which is a medicine all its own. Self-care is critical to the success of your family but can be hard to come by for special-needs families. We have so many demands and emergencies to deal with that it can be difficult to make time; even so, don't neglect being proactive in this area or you'll be left with your defenses down.

Psalm 23 tells us that the Good Shepherd "makes" us lie down in green pastures, leads us beside quiet waters, and refreshes and restores our soul. Self-care isn't just "nice to have." It's essential and necessary, and it must be intentional and focused. No special-needs family has time to waste on things that don't reinvigorate or promote life. Be sure that if you're taking a break from professional or family duties, you're doing something that makes you a better husband and dad.

For years my favorite "decompression chamber" was the pool. We were fortunate enough to be able to install one at our old house when I was still in the corporate world. It was my oasis. I couldn't wait to finish my workday so that Jon Alex and I could have some float time. It was essential to my well-being, and it restored my soul. It was also a way for me to have some hang time with Jon Alex. I will always be grateful for those years I was able to enjoy that gift.

Here is a practical idea to help you oversee the self-care of your family. Call a family meeting and ask each person to write a list of five to seven free or low-cost activities they enjoy that would restore and refresh them. Assign everyone the task of watching out for each other and making sure no one is feeling overly stressed. When someone is struggling, help them choose an activity from their list and make it happen. Teach your children how to deal with stress by your example. Talk openly about ways in which you cope with worry, and identify what works best for each member.

Watch and Pray

To be a successful special-needs father, you must be aware of the overall condition of your family. It's your job to know how each person is doing emotionally, physically, and spiritually. In Matthew 26:41, Jesus encourages us to "watch and pray so that you will not fall into temptation. The spirit is willing, but the flesh is weak." Like a good platoon leader, a father is always watching to see whether anyone is in trouble. Dads are also praying for the health and well-being of the family unit. Men, it's your duty to be praying daily for your family. It's essential that you do so. Make it a priority to check in with each person in your family every few days. Ask them specific questions about how they're doing. Here are some examples:

- What was the best/worst thing about your day?
- Did anything happen today that made you excited/happy/afraid/angry?
- Tell me something about you that I don't know.
- Was this a "do-over" day or a "Let's do that again" day? In what ways?

Let your family know that you're praying for them. Tell them that you're watching over them and asking God to protect them. The world has become an increasingly scary place, and your family needs to know that their leader is protecting them with prayer. Asking about their feelings will help all of you stay connected. Children who feel seen and heard are much less likely to rebel. All of us need this recognition, so lead by example. Let them know you're there for them, watching and praying. Talking about feelings and emotions isn't always easy for men, but you must push through and connect at a heart level with your wife and children. Otherwise, everyone will feel adrift and will go their own way. Keep them close and safe by watching, listening, and praying.

Search the Scriptures

A powerful way to fortify your family is to search God's Word for truths that apply specifically to them. Having your family covered in prayer is vital, but covering them in Scripture affords a whole new level of protection. There are times when it feels as though all of hell is conspiring against us. If you feel that you're under spiritual attack, you can read this Scripture aloud over your family: "'No weapon formed against you shall prosper, and every tongue which rises against you in judgment you shall condemn. This is the heritage of the servants of the LORD, and their righteousness is from Me,' says the LORD" (Isaiah 54:17 NKJV). Psalm 59:1 is helpful too: "Deliver me from my enemies, O God; be my fortress against those who are attacking me." There are verses for all kinds of situations you will face, and declaring them out loud will bring peace and confidence to your family.

Having your family covered in prayer is vital, but covering them in Scripture affords a whole new level of protection.

Another way you can fortify your family with Scripture is to identify a life verse for each person. A life verse is a Scripture you believe God has assigned to you or your child. To discover what this life verse is, simply ask God to reveal the guiding Scripture for your child's life or your own. Patiently listen, and if you don't get an answer the first time, continue watching and listening. The Lord will point to something if you keep asking.

My wife's sister tells the story of how she was able to identify her children's life verses. My sister-in-law was very ill and feeling exhausted. Not knowing what was wrong with her, she cried out to God for help. He led her to Luke 1:76–80, the story of the meeting of Mary and Elizabeth, who were both pregnant at the time. The specific verses talked about John the Baptist being born and becoming a prophet. Later that day she learned that she was pregnant with her first child, and the Lord showed her that this was to be the child's life passage. With her second child, the Lord assigned a verse that was the theme of a yearlong Bible study in which she was participating during the first year of that child's life.

No matter how old your child is, you can always seek God about a life verse for him or her. These verses help you know your child better and can guide you as you make decisions. These are the two Scriptures we claim over Jon Alex: "'Neither this man nor his parents sinned,' said Jesus, 'but this happened so that the works of God might be displayed in him'" (John 9:3) and "We know that in all things God works for the good of those who love him, who have been called according to his purpose" (Romans 8:28). These Scriptures have deep meaning for us as a family, and we display them in our home.

I encourage you to speak Scripture aloud in your home. Display verses that encourage you and remind you of God's faithfulness. Declare God's truth over your people. Open yourself up to God, and he will show you great things that will bless and protect your family. Search the Scriptures on behalf of your family, and you will strengthen your home.

Speak Life

Proverbs 18:21 declares that "the tongue has the power of life and death." Dads, your words contain the power either to give life or to crush your children. Think about that. You can speak life over your family, or you can kill them with your words. Of all the behaviors and actions that can fortify a family, this is one of the most important.

Words matter. Dads, you have got to be speaking words of life over your children every day. Your kids will believe whatever you say about them. Your child will become whatever he or she believes, and what they believe about themselves will be determined by what you speak over them. Make it a point on a daily basis to speak positive words that affirm your child.

I continually make an effort to speak affirmations over my son and my wife. I know how important this is now, though I didn't at first. I let years go by during which I could have been building our foundation as a family, but I kept silent, protecting myself and wasting this great opportunity. Now I tell Jon Alex how proud I am to be his dad and how honored I am that God chose him to be my son. Some people might think that he can't understand me, but I know for certain that his spirit hears every word I say.

You *come from Love to be love* in this weary world.

What if speaking this way isn't your style? Did your father speak life over you, or did he crush you with his words? If this way of relating is foreign to you, don't worry. Learning to speak positive blessings is like anything else. It takes practice. At first it will feel extremely awkward. You may not be very good at it. The words won't flow, and it will be hard to think of affirmations to share. Don't let that stop you from trying. This process is like drawing water. You have to prime the pump for a while before you'll get any water. Ask God to open the reservoir inside you of his love for your family. Start trying to speak positive things as they come to you. Your family may wonder what has happened to you, but don't let awkwardness stop you. Within a short time, you'll develop a flow of thoughts and words that you didn't know were inside you. If you keep practicing, you'll find blessings and positive words coming to you with ease. Yes, the process can be a little uncomfortable, but it will turn you into a pipeline of love for your family. You'll become a source of love because you're depending on the one true source for help. He'll supply everything you need.

This journey as the parent of a child with special needs can be grueling, giving us ample opportunity to be negative, joyless, and careless with our words. I get it. You don't always feel joyful. You don't always revel in your child's autistic behavior or physical challenges or the continual needs you face. It's hard to stay positive, but you have a well of goodness and love from which you can draw. It isn't sourced in this world but from the center of God, the center of Love. Try to remember that you *come from Love to be love* in this weary world. Use your mouth to speak powerful blessings over your family. Pour out love on them, and they will thrive!

Here are a few blessings straight from Scripture to get you started:

> The Lord bless you and keep you; the Lord make his face shine on you and be gracious to you; the Lord turn his face toward you and give you peace. (Numbers 6:24–26)
>
> Be strong and courageous. Do not be afraid; do not be discouraged, for the Lord your God will be with you wherever you go. (Joshua 1:9)
>
> Trust in the Lord with all your heart and lean not on your own understanding; in all your ways submit to him, and he will make your paths straight. (Proverbs 3:5–6)

Approve

Why do you think little boys yell for their dads to watch them attempt a great feat like jumping a ditch on their bike, throwing a football, or leaping out of a swing? Because in the heart of every little boy there is a deep and compelling desire to earn his father's love and respect. Do you remember that feeling, wanting so much to please your dad? Begging for his approval and attention with every trick and skill you could lay before him? "Watch this, Dad, watch this!"

We all desperately need the approval of our dads. I remember this well from my own childhood. My dad had been a great basketball player, so I wanted to be one too. I wanted to please him and make him proud. My dad coached my high school basketball team, in fact. I was good enough to start on the varsity team, but we both knew I would never be great. I was always secretly afraid I had disappointed him, but he never made me feel like a disappointment.

No matter how old we get, deep down inside we still want our father's approval and respect. This is one measurement that assures us that we have become men in our own right. Did your father give you his blessing? Did he approve of you? If not, I strongly encourage you to seek the approval of your heavenly Father. His respect trumps all. Think about your father's impact on your life and determine to give your children even better than what you received as a child. It's critical for their success to feel your approval of them.

My dad is a man of few words. While I was growing up, he seldom vocalized his love for his kids, but his actions left no doubt about where he stood. He was always there for us, always engaged in our lives. Some time ago he sent me a card out of the blue. Inside he had written, "Just wanted you to know that you are the best son a dad could ever have." I cried for ten minutes after I read it. That card remains priceless to me. It's the best gift he could ever have given me. I keep it in the front drawer of my desk and reread it often. What he is really saying to me is, "I love you because you're my son." Period. Nothing else matters. I have his respect and validation because I'm his son.

I love Jon Alex in the exact same way. Once when Becky and I were interviewed, the question was asked, "What do you most enjoy about your son with special needs?" I thought about this for a moment and then replied, "What I enjoy most is the simple fact that he's my son. There is nothing he can do to make me love him more. He's the best son I could ask for because he's a gift to me." God's love for you is just the same. You don't have to prove yourself or make the grade to be loved. You simply have to let him love you; the real joy comes when you love him back.[13]

If you want to fortify and strengthen your family, let them know you like them (yes, I said *like* them). Let them know you approve of them. Don't hold things over their heads or demand certain behaviors before you'll be willing to release your love. That's control! Often when we give them what they need, they'll soon become what you want anyway. You must lead in the giving of love. This is what God does.

Gather

To strengthen your family, you must come together. In this frantic age of going and doing, in which busyness has become an idol, it's easy to neglect simply being together. You can't create deep bonds, foster mutual respect, or impart wisdom if you aren't together. I urge you to look at your family schedule. Don't succumb to the pressure to always be on the go. Find time every week to gather together as a united family. Make this an expectation for everyone. Set a regular time and stick to it. Use this time to discuss family business, forecast the schedule for the coming week, reward family members who have achieved goals or done well, and have fun together.

Assign the members of your family rotating tasks, such as secretary, timekeeper, leader, and game warden (the person who picks the game). Encourage everyone to listen well. You can establish ground rules and give someone the role of referee. If rules are broken, give them a red flag to throw. The more fun you make it and the more power your kids feel they have in the family meeting, the more they'll buy into the process.

There are many products on the market that can help you start conversations. There are boxes of cards that prompt worthwhile discussion and games that will help you connect as a family. Let your time together include both deep discussion and lots of laughter. It's in such times that you cement who you are as a family. You can perform your family cheer and recite your family motto. As the leader, you can discuss one important trait to which you want your children to aspire, or share something you learned that week.

Being vulnerable during these times is essential. Let your children see your heart. Apologize if you need to, or confess a shortfall for which you need prayer. Let them see how you're feeling and know that you're real. Family meetings are also an opportunity for you to see *them* and assess how they're doing. Ask probing questions or play "show and tell" together. Before the meeting, ask everyone to bring something that's important to them or share something that represents the family to them, then ask them to explain why. Be aware that the older your kids are when you start the routine of family meetings, the tougher it may be to get them to participate.

Here are some ideas for family meeting topics:

1. If we could be the very best possible family, what would that look like and what would we be doing?
2. How can we make this household run more smoothly?
3. How can we save money now to enjoy later (the importance of delayed gratification)?
4. Who do you admire and why?
5. What are your greatest gifts and weaknesses?
6. What goals should we set for this year?
7. How can you be a better you?
8. Who can you trust?

Obviously, you'll need to adapt the topics to fit your family, but consider topics that will help you know and understand each other better. Give family meetings a try. Don't allow initial resistance from any of your children, or even yourself, to keep you from fortifying your family by gathering together.

If your family is able, I would also highly recommend doing service projects together. Our family is involved in many events that support special-needs families, and it strengthens us to work together. Find a local place to volunteer, or locate another special-needs family that needs support. Show up to rake leaves, clean the garage, or whatever it is they need. Working together as a family to help others is a significant way to teach service and strengthen your core.

Let's SMEAC a hypothetical family service project to give you a feel for what that might look like. Remember that SMEAC is a tool to help you be a better leader. Special-needs families have to prepare before we do anything. Sometimes we need to scope out a situation to see whether it will accommodate our family. A little planning and preparation before an outing go a long way toward ensuring a better experience for everyone.

Situation

In our last family meeting we decided to volunteer at the local animal shelter. They need help cleaning cages and organizing food donations. Our family loves dogs, and we have always tried to support shelters in our area. The problem has been that our son Mason, who has autism, has sensory issues that make the chaos of a shelter hard to deal with. He gets anxious and can have outbursts when he's overstimulated. Taking him on this kind of outing is always a roll of the dice. The good news is that the shelter is also looking for people to help them advertise adoptable dogs on social media. Mason is a natural with the computer and would love posting pictures on social media. He can do this from the car, if necessary. This project allows all of us to participate, which means that everyone will get to serve in some way. We're scheduled to go next Saturday to volunteer from 1–3 p.m.

Mission

Our family will bond and become stronger by serving our community in a way we're all passionate about. We will help the local animal shelter and attempt to get some puppies placed in the homes of families we know.

Execution

- We will meet as a family at noon on Saturday to go over our plan for this service project.
- Roles will be assigned according to ability and desire. The kids will clean cages and organize food, while Mason and Dad work the social media angle.

- We will depart at 12:40 p.m. for the ten-minute drive to the shelter.
- We will take a donation of dog food and a list of prospective homes for the animals.
- We will dress casually for cleaning and will take snacks for the kids to enjoy when we're finished.

Administration

- Gas up the van and make sure everyone has proper clothing for cleaning.
- Purchase dog food for donation.
- Provide a list of people who might want to adopt. Take computer and phone for pictures and uploads to social media.
- Prepare snacks and drinks.
- Pray during the week that we will bless the shelter and grow closer as a family.

Command

- Gas up the van and purchase dog food—Dad
- Make sure children are dressed and prepared for the project—Mom and Dad
- Prepare snacks and drinks—Mom and Amy
- Prepare list of potential adopters—All
- Bring computer and phone—Mason
- Pray for successful volunteering—All

Encouragement from the Homefront . . . A Letter from Becky

Brave Soldier,

I am truly grateful for all the ways you work to strengthen your family. I know they appreciate it too. One of the greatest responsibilities you have is to encourage and cheer your people on. The special-needs life can be brutal for every member of the family.

As the leader of your home, you can set the tone for how everyone behaves and treats each other. You set the example and it flows to the rest of the family.

Jeff was a great encourager in his later years, but he struggled early on. He would have been the first to tell you that he used to have a hard time telling people "Thank you." I don't know why that was, but he would say that in the early years he was very self-absorbed. Later, when the "breaking"—his physical deterioration—began, his heart softened and changed.

Toward the end of his life, I had to do a lot of caregiving for Jeff. Every night before bed he would say, "Thank you for all you did for me today." He told me often how beautiful he thought I was and that I was even more beautiful to him than when we were first married. Guys, these are words a woman needs to hear from her man.

A week before he died, Jeff sent me flowers when Jon Alex was in the hospital. The card read, "You are never more beautiful than when you are taking care of our son." I can't remember when he ever seemed jealous of the time I spent taking care of Jon Alex. He loved and appreciated what I did for our son.

Jeff spoke life over us. As a couple, we made it a point never to speak negatively about each other in public. If he and I were upset with one another, no one else knew about it. We kept our family matters private. So many people want to hash things out in public, but that can cause humiliation and division. There are times when we need to seek the counsel of others, but there are also times when we need to quietly wait. Jeff and I decided to protect and defend each other. This was a decision we made to safeguard our marriage. We didn't do this well early in our marriage, but we learned how critical it was after Jon Alex was born. After that we made it a priority, and it brought strength to our marriage.

Gentlemen, use your power as a good and loving man to build a strong and healthy family. Pray for your people, encourage them, and give them your approval every chance you get. Gather them together and bless them with your words. Keep a lookout for anything that will try to destroy the peace and unity of your family. Your strength is their strength.

Blessings from the Homefront,
Becky

MISSION CRITICAL

- ☐ Commit in your mind and heart to doing all you can to fortify and strengthen your family.
- ☐ Set goals for yourself related to the topics introduced in this chapter, and make a written plan to achieve each of them over the course of the year: engage in self-care, watch and pray, search the Scriptures, speak life, approve, and gather.
- ☐ Build up your own inner man daily through reading the Word of God and praying so that you'll remain fit to lead.

CHAPTER 7

Equip

To equip is to train and prepare. Equipping someone makes them ready for a specific task and provides them with the tools needed to complete that job. Life in the military is heavily focused on training and equipping soldiers so they'll be prepared to face any scenario with confidence. This is our job as fathers as well. We must prepare our children for the future and equip them to deal with the challenges that lie ahead. We are the ones who prepare them for life. As you move through this chapter, think about your own father. Did he equip you well? What impact did his parenting have on you? How can you do better for your own children?

This significant task can be particularly daunting with a child who has special needs. Some of you, like me, know that your child will be in your care for their lifetime. Others of you have relatively high-functioning children who have the hope of living independently in the world with a little help. The demands our children will face in life will differ according to each child's situation, but there are some foundational truths that remain in place, regardless of their challenges.

EQUIPPING YOUR FAMILY

During his time on earth, Jesus was quite outspoken about his ambitious desire to equip people. He was abundantly clear about what he intended to do in his mission statement. Listen carefully to his words:

> The scroll of the prophet Isaiah was handed to him. Unrolling it, he found the place where it is written:

> "The Spirit of the Lord is on me,
> because he has anointed me
> to proclaim good news to the poor.
> He has sent me to proclaim freedom for the prisoners
> and recovery of sight for the blind,
> to set the oppressed free,
> to proclaim the year of the Lord's favor."
>
> Then he rolled up the scroll, gave it back to the attendant and sat down. The eyes of everyone in the synagogue were fastened on him. He began by saying to them, "Today this scripture is fulfilled in your hearing." (Luke 4:17–21)

Jesus knew that he was here to liberate people and show them how to live in union with God. His mission was to release people from their bondage, help them rise above their circumstances, and equip them for life. He believed in restoration and hope for all of us, and he is our example of how to equip people for life.

Before you discount his example as too difficult for mere mortals, let me remind you that you have access to the same power source Jesus did. It was the Spirit of God who made him able to do these great things. He also told us in John 14:12 that we would do the same and *even greater* things than he did. Let that sink in. We're called to do the same work as Jesus with the same power source he had.

As you prepare to equip your children for life, remember that it is God who will supply whatever it is you need to teach them. It is his power that will make your words and instruction come alive to them. Each time you instruct your children, ask the Lord to translate what you're saying into their hearts and minds so that it is enlivened with his power. This is particularly important to do with our kids who are developmentally delayed. Their spirits can comprehend more than their minds can retain. Ask God to translate your instruction as truth in their hearts. Teach even the most impaired children the truth of God's Word. They've been created in his image and will recognize the "mother tongue" of God's Word in their spirits.

There is no possible way to anticipate all the challenges that will come to our kids in their lifetimes. We can't be there to help every time they have a problem. We must train them to be ready to face life as independently as possible. To equip our children for life, there are three questions we need to help them answer. If they know these truths, they will know how to respond to any challenge they face. These questions are:

1. Who is my source? (Source)
2. Who am I? (Self)
3. What am I here to do? (Service)

If we instill within our children this foundation, they will be equipped to seek God in any situation. Only God can provide everything they need. We will never be enough. If they know source, self, and service, they have a template for life in Christ. This is a priceless gift to give your children, a real-time road map for their journey.

WHO IS MY SOURCE?

This question is the foundation upon which everything else rests. Our whole paradigm for living is based on how we answer this one question. If you truly believe that there's a God who cares for you, that he is *for* you and has your best interest at heart, this will impact the way you interpret everything that happens to you in this life.

It's your responsibility as a follower of Christ to teach your children about the one true source. As you live out your life in front of them, you're teaching them who and what you believe. If you're reading this and don't believe in God, I invite you to stop right now and ask him to reveal himself to you. If you find yourself somewhere between full faith in God and unbelief, then let these truths speak to you and ground you more deeply.

Your children need to know that God is our one true source for:

- Wisdom
- Protection
- Provision

If your children know and love God and know their own purpose, they can turn to him for wisdom no matter what trials may come. God will always be there for your children, even if you can't be. If you're unsure whether your child can make a conscious decision for Christ, teach them the truth anyway and trust that the Holy Spirit will translate. You need not fear for them. God knows their heart, just as he knows yours. We read Bible stories to Jon Alex and surround him with music and uplifting messages. We pray with him and share our faith openly, trusting God to convey the truth to his heart. I believe with the full weight of my conviction that while Jon Alex's body may be "broken," his spirit is perfectly intact. Every child has the right to know the truth.

God will always be there for your children, even if you can't be.

Our children also need to know this important fact: in the kingdom of God, things work a bit backward. It is often said that seeing is believing, but with God, believing is required before we see the outcome of the situation we are praying about. God asks us to believe and trust him when we cannot even imagine how he will work things out. He also asks us to trust him when things don't go the way we had hoped.

Hebrews 11:6 puts it this way: "Without faith it is impossible to please God, because anyone who comes to him must believe that he exists and that he rewards those who earnestly seek him." You must first believe that God exists and then trust that he'll reward you if you truly seek him. It's only then that his wisdom, protection, and provision will be made clear to you. If you must "see it" in order to believe it, you'll never grow in your relationship with God. He will never be real to you until you decide to suspend your disbelief and take the leap of faith.

Dads, if you haven't taken that leap to fully trust God, now is the time. You're going to need him and everything he can provide for you. So will your children. Many of you attend church, live a good life, and care about good things, but if you don't let yourself truly believe, you won't enjoy the riches that a life lived in relationship with God has to offer. Ask God to reveal himself to you and put people in your life who can help lead you closer to him. This will make all the difference in your future.

One of the great blessings about having and knowing kids with special needs is that they tend to be a little less stuck in the "real world" and a little closer to understanding the things of God. They often give love freely and easily. They tend to see the deeper things that we miss because they keep things simple. In fact, they may have an easier time accepting their faith than you do. Learn from them. They're here to teach us.

I can't begin to tell you the endless lessons my son has taught me. He lives in a place of peace and unity with God. How do I know? Because that peace radiates from him. The tenderness of God comes through him and humbles me time and again. Don't think for one second that, because your child is nonverbal or severely impaired, she can't know God. My son is a living testimony to the fact that these children can. Teach them truth and learn from their natural inclination toward God.

Wisdom

When you share with your children that God is their source, let them know that he will give us wisdom whenever we need it. Wisdom is the insight and guidance we need to live well. The first chapter of James clearly instructs us to ask God for wisdom and assures us that it will be given. But when we ask, we must believe that our request will be honored. Any time we ask or believe God for something but leave open the back door of doubt, we're being double-minded. A double-minded person is unstable and feels tossed around by life. We must be fully committed in our faith in order to be effective.

> If any of you lacks wisdom, you should ask God, who gives generously to all without finding fault, and it will be given to you. But when you ask, you must believe and not doubt, because the one who doubts is like a wave of the sea, blown and tossed by the wind. That person should not expect to receive anything from the Lord. Such a person is double-minded and unstable in all they do. (James 1:5–8)

Pray with your children and ask God to give them wisdom and understanding. Watch their lives carefully, and praise them openly for decisions that reflect wisdom. Let them know when you see them acting in ways consistent with godly understanding. Encourage the pursuit of wisdom and teach them to search for it. It's a pearl of great price. Listen to the words of King Solomon, one of the wisest men to ever live, on the moral benefits of wisdom:

> My son, if you accept my words
> and store up my commands within you,
> turning your ear to wisdom
> and applying your heart to understanding—
> indeed, if you call out for insight
> and cry aloud for understanding,
> and if you look for it as for silver
> and search for it as for hidden treasure,
> then you will understand the fear of the LORD
> and find the knowledge of God.
> For the LORD gives wisdom;
> from his mouth come knowledge and understanding.
> He holds success in store for the upright,
> he is a shield to those whose walk is blameless,
> for he guards the course of the just
> and protects the way of his faithful ones.
>
> Then you will understand what is right and just
> and fair—every good path.

> For wisdom will enter your heart,
>   and knowledge will be pleasant to your soul.
> Discretion will protect you,
>   and understanding will guard you.
> (Proverbs 2:1–11)

Wisdom teaches us how to walk with God, how to live, and how to maintain our integrity in a treacherous world. It's essential that we equip our children with an understanding of their need for wisdom and how to get it: they must simply ask.

Protection

God is also our source of protection—our rock, our shield, and our fortress. To a kid in the twenty-first century, it might make more sense to say that he's stronger, faster, smarter, and braver than any superhero. Not to mention that he's for real! Read to your family the beautiful opening words of Psalm 18 and be reminded of his strength and power to protect us.

Children are often tormented by fear. From the very beginning the Enemy of our souls comes to frighten us. Fear is dangerous because it steals our inner peace. This peace is essential to our being able to hear and follow God. Things like nightmares, trauma, and scary television shows can lodge in a child's heart and unsettle him or her. Don't belittle your children for being afraid. Many times such fear is an actual attack of the Enemy. Teach them instead to focus and fight! Teaching them a few simple verses to recite aloud can help combat fear. Here are two examples:

> The Lord is my light and my salvation—whom shall I fear? The Lord is the stronghold of my life—of whom shall I be afraid? (Psalm 27:1)

> When I'm afraid, I put my trust in you. I trust in God. I praise his word. I trust in God. I am not afraid. What can mere people do to me? (Psalm 56:3–4 NIRV)

It's important to train our children to combat fear. This may not seem like a big deal, but fear can completely derail us. Think about it: you let the tiniest bit of fear take hold in your mind, and before you know it, that fear has taken over. At first, it's just a little fear, but then you become discouraged and in no time find yourself doubting the goodness of God. This has happened to me so many times during my health struggles. I understand the power of fear to dismantle our faith. Don't tolerate it in your own mind, and teach your children to fight it with prayer, Scripture, and faith.

Let me tell you about a very real battle Becky and I have fought with fear. You may know what this feels like. When you have a child who is nonverbal and requires hands-on care for all their needs, it can be extremely scary to allow someone else to care for them—even a trusted friend. This is especially true when you must put your trust in the local school system and people you don't know to provide personal care. It's so easy to allow fear to overtake you. We began early in our son's life to pray that God would place his best people in Jon Alex's classroom—people who would be well equipped to help him. We prayed for them to have creative thoughts and new ideas about his education and care. We also asked that if someone came into the situation who was *not* best for Jon Alex, God would remove them. We asked that God would reveal anything that we needed to know about anyone working with our son.

Because of those prayers we were able to find our peace. As change after change would happen in his school, we were able to remain calm and trust that God was moving the pieces around as needed. Because we had prayed in advance about all this, we trusted that the changes would be good for our son, and they always were. There were times when a change didn't seem to make sense, but later we would invariably see that it had been for the best.

Many times parents want to fight the system when changes arise, because we think we know what's best for our child. Our early days in the school system were much more stressful when we were trying to control everything. When we let go and trusted God, our family had much more peace. It was amazing that many times when there were things going on that Jon Alex couldn't communicate, God would send someone to tell us. We called them our "little birds." God would send them our way to fill us in on things we needed to know. We must realize that we can't always be with our children and that the best protection for them is a God who is ever present.

Provision

In chapter 5 we explored the idea that God is our one true source. He is the river of provision upon which we must depend. Philippians 4:19 says that he will supply all—not just some—of our needs. Our children need to know that God is their provider. They need to be taught that he will meet their needs and lovingly provide for them. The thing is that you can't teach what you don't believe. Trust me, they will understand it's all just words if you say it but don't live it.

So how can you teach them if you're still working on this one yourself? Watch for an opportunity to come together as a family and trust God to provide. Begin to live out your faith in front of your kids. Start small and build your faith together. God is eager to build a relationship with you, but that means that you have to be vulnerable and open. Tell him what you really need and ask him to show up for you.

Live out your faith in front of your kids. Start small and build your faith together.

I'll leave you with a reminder about provision. In the Lord's Prayer, Jesus asks the Father to "give us this day our daily bread." In the Hebrew mind, the day began at sundown, making this a request for provision from one sundown to the next. In other words, "Give us enough for tonight through tomorrow afternoon." One day's worth of provision is all Jesus asked for. In the American culture, that seems ridiculous. Most of us want fully stocked cupboards and the luxury of knowing that there is plenty to spare. We buy in bulk and feel the liberty to throw out anything that doesn't meet our high standards. We want a savings account that leaves us feeling satisfied and comfortable. We want to accrue, purchase, accumulate, and build our financial empire. We want more than we need, but we are taught by Jesus to ask for just enough. We think "mega" . . . and God responds with manna—*daily* bread.

That isn't to say that God doesn't give exceedingly and abundantly, far beyond what we could ask or imagine—because he does. But it is a paradigm shift for most Christians in the developed world to realize that if we're taken care of for today and tomorrow, then we've been given our daily bread. It's a temptation to want the security of having more than we actually need. We must remember that our idea of what we "need" is more in line with what our culture says than what God says. People who love and worship him in other parts of the globe live on much less than we do. My point is this: if you ask for daily bread and receive it, you've been blessed. Our hope is in our God, not in our stuff.

WHO AM I?

The next essential question we must help our children answer is, "Who am I?" Having a solid sense of who they are helps equip our children for the tumultuous world they will face. We all have a deeply rooted need to feel grounded and secure, to know who we are in relation to the world around us. This is even more important for children with special needs, who are often treated as outsiders and rejected by the mainstream world.

At Rising Above Ministries, we have a mantra about our special kids. It appears on our T-shirts and in our literature: "Wonderfully made, created for a plan and a purpose, destined to glorify God." We speak these words over them again and again because we believe it. This is who our children are.

Wonderfully Made

> You created my inmost being; you knit me together in my mother's womb. I praise you because I am fearfully and won-

> derfully made; your works are wonderful, I know that full well. My frame was not hidden from you when I was made in the secret place, when I was woven together in the depths of the earth. Your eyes saw my unformed body; all the days ordained for me were written in your book before one of them came to be. (Psalm 139:13–16)

This truth will change you if you let it. God saw us and our children still unformed in the womb. He ordained our days on this earth before we ever got here. We are indeed fearfully and wonderfully made—just as we are. Crooked teeth, crazy hair, limbs that don't work, eyes that need glasses, legs that will never walk—he is the Lord of it all. This doesn't sit well with our perfectionistic culture, in which we're made to feel "less than" if we don't pass certain standards. The truth is that we're fearfully and wonderfully made—and your kids need to know it!

Created for a Plan and a Purpose

"'For I know the plans I have for you,' declares the LORD, 'plans to prosper you and not to harm you, plans to give you hope and a future.'" These words from Jeremiah 29:11 afford us hope whenever we feel lost and uncertain. Your children need to know and believe the truth that God has a plan and purpose for their lives too, no matter how impaired they may be. Jon Alex has never spoken a word, yet his life has inspired thousands of people and has been a help to so many, not the least of whom is me. God sent him here with a plan and a purpose. Jon Alex is my own personal bridge to bring me closer to the heart of Christ. Living with him and loving him has been the primary means by which God has apprehended my heart. I daresay I would not have been able to say this if he had been typical. Never let your kids think they don't have purpose. Foster their understanding of destiny. Talk to them about God's plan for their lives. Help them believe the truth that they matter. This will equip them to stand strong when they feel weakest and least secure.

Destined to Glorify God

"The Son is the radiance of God's glory and the exact representation of his being, sustaining all things by his powerful word. After he had provided purification for sins, he sat down at the right hand of the Majesty in heaven" (Hebrews 1:3). This verse identifies Jesus as being in himself the radiance of God's glory. But you and I also glorify God when we walk in truth and righteousness. We are sons and daughters of God. It's our destiny to glorify God, and it's vital for us to teach our children that they have a destiny to bring glory to him. Their lives matter—and so does yours.

I am fearfully and wonderfully made, created for a plan and a purpose, and destined to glorify God: these truths are the foundation of genuine self-esteem. Self-esteem that is rooted in "self" will fail because each of us knows all too well how empty we really are. But self-esteem based on who we are in Christ—now *that* will hold. I'm here to share a highly effective way for us to impact our children's lives. If we soak ourselves in the truth, we'll soon see a difference in the way we think and live. I strongly recommend that you help your children with a daily dose of truth. It should be administered as faithfully as daily medications.

Here's the idea. Create a list like the one below that is specific to the needs of each child. Post it on the bathroom mirror or in some other place where they'll see it daily. If at all possible, read it with them daily. If your child can't read or is severely impaired, declare these truths aloud over them every day. Watch as they gradually transform into a better version of themselves because the truth will set their hearts free, strengthen their spirits, and equip them for life:

I Am

1. I am a prince/princess, a child of the King (1 John 3:1).
2. I am radically loved by God (Romans 5:8).
3. I am fearfully and wonderfully made (Psalm 139:14).
4. I know God has a plan and a purpose for my life (Jeremiah 29:11).
5. I matter (Jeremiah 31:3).

6. I am focused on what is good and true (Philippians 4:8).
7. I am safe and sound in God (Isaiah 54:17).
8. I am an overcomer—I get knocked down, but I get up again (Romans 8:37).
9. I am not afraid because God is with me (Psalm 118:6).
10. I am fulfilling my destiny in Jesus Christ (Psalm 138:8)!

A daily dose of these truths will make a lasting impression on your children. You might consider making a list for yourself too. We're never too old to be transformed by God's Word.

WHAT AM I HERE TO DO?

Now we shift to the final question, "What am I here to do?" Knowing the answer to this question is critical to your child's understanding of life. Your children need to know that they exist to reflect the image of God. Genesis 1:27 says that we are created in God's image. We're the image bearers of God! This image, however, is marred when we enter the fallen world. It's subject to the brokenness of the world into which we're born. The beauty of being redeemed by Jesus is that it allows us to recover the destiny we were born to fulfill. We can become true image bearers—spreaders of God's love and goodness to all humankind.

As our example, Jesus showed us that we can be image bearers of God, just as he is. We are to humbly serve and give our lives away to those who need us, just as he did. Although Jesus had every right to, he never behaved as though he were better or more entitled than others. He was the King, but he chose to behave as a humble servant. He reflected God's servant heart in taking this stance. But he was at the same time fierce and forward thinking. He wasn't weak or wishy-washy but was bold and courageous. When it came to others, he was willing to take a position of service. That was his strength. If you're a servant leader, you understand that to humbly serve takes far more courage and self-control than to be a modern-day "It's all about me" type of leader.

Throughout our lives on planet Earth, the Enemy does everything he can to get us to gaze into the reflective mirror, to become distracted by our own image and make life all about us. He hopes that we'll seek our own image instead of God's. Jesus teaches us to flip the mirror to reflect God and pry our focus away from ourselves. The life of a special-needs dad isn't easy, but reversing the mirror can help. If you allow the gift of your child to help you break your addiction to yourself and your own image, it will help you fulfill your destiny and become a reflection of God instead.

Teach your children that they're here to show the world what God looks like. They're here to reflect his glory by being who they were created to be. It isn't as hard as we try to make it. Every created thing in some way reflects the glory of God. Think about the mountains and the trees. They testify to God's greatness just by being what they were created to be. If we live our lives with hearts focused on God, we will naturally reflect his glory—we'll show a little bit of his goodness to the world. This is no cause for pride; we're simply reflecting what is already shining in us. Teach your kids to shine!

ARMOR UP DAILY

We opened this chapter with the definition of equipping, which is to train and prepare someone, providing them with the tools needed to complete their job. One of the most essential tools God has given us is spiritual armor. We often forget that we are living in the middle of an epic spiritual battle, and we need to be armed for the fight. This armor, while invisible, is very real. I believe it is essential to successful Christian living and should be applied daily to have its full effect. The sixth chapter of Ephesians teaches us about the armor of God, and we are instructed to put it on so we can stand against the deception of the Enemy.

> Finally, be strong in the Lord and in his mighty power. Put on the full armor of God, so that you can take your stand against the devil's schemes. For our struggle is not against flesh and blood, but against the rulers, against the authorities, against the powers of this dark world and against the spiritual forces

> of evil in the heavenly realms. Therefore put on the full armor of God, so that when the day of evil comes, you may be able to stand your ground, and after you have done everything, to stand. Stand firm then, with the belt of truth buckled around your waist, with the breastplate of righteousness in place, and with your feet fitted with the readiness that comes from the gospel of peace. In addition to all this, take up the shield of faith, with which you can extinguish all the flaming arrows of the evil one. Take the helmet of salvation and the sword of the Spirit, which is the word of God.
>
> And pray in the Spirit on all occasions with all kinds of prayers and requests. With this in mind, be alert and always keep on praying for all the Lord's people. (vv. 10–18)

I encourage you to make putting on the armor a part of your spiritual routine for yourself and your family. You can make it a game with your kids to "apply" the armor each and every day. Learn each piece and what it protects, and teach them to suit up before they leave the house. You wouldn't go out without shoes or a shirt. Don't go out without your armor either.

Here's a quick summary of the armor and its purpose. I highly recommend that you study the significance of each piece on your own to get a full understanding of its vast importance in our lives.

Belt of Truth

Placed around the waist, it protects our core and helps us remember the truth. It confronts the lies of the Enemy.

Breastplate of Righteousness

Over the chest, the breastplate protects us from shame and diminishment. It's the truth of Christ's righteousness over our hearts.

Shoes of Peace

With these shoes we have a firm foundation and can walk in peace, bringing it wherever we go.

Shield of Faith

This full body shield is at our disposal when we activate our faith and walk in that knowledge. It protects us from the attacks of the Enemy and shelters us from his fiery darts.

Helmet of Salvation

Placed on our heads, this helmet protects our minds and gives us the great security of knowing that our salvation is at work 24/7.

Sword of the Spirit

Our one offensive weapon, the sword of the Spirit is the Word of God. There is no stronger weapon against the wiles of the Enemy. God's Word defends and protects us.

Let's go through another hypothetical SMEAC, this time to address one of the toughest times of day: getting out the door in the morning. I know it's hard to imagine adding another thing to your morning routine, but just think about the power and confidence your family would gain by being fully equipped for the day before you all go your separate ways.

Situation

Our family has a tough morning schedule, with everyone leaving at different times, but I want to send them off each day feeling covered in prayer and empowered to face what comes. I want to initiate a "Family Focus" time each morning, which will last ten minutes. It will take some getting used to, but I believe we can make it part of our daily routine. I think Mom will be happy to get on board, but our ten-year-old, Jason, will likely resist. His younger brother, Michael, our child with Down syndrome, will require a special task to get him invested.

Mission

Our family will meet every morning for ten minutes to focus on the plan for the day, to pray, and to build our foundation as a family. My personal focus will be to equip all family members with wisdom and encouragement and to cover them in prayer.

Execution

- Michael will be given a bell to ring at 6:45 a.m. to call the family together.
- We will meet at the kitchen table, and a ten-minute timer will be set by Jason, who will be our timekeeper.
- Each person will briefly share what is scheduled to happen in their day and what they need prayer for. Mom will forecast the events of the evening.
- All others will listen quietly, and Mom will make brief meeting notes in our family notebook.
- We will each pray for the person on our right, and Dad will close the prayer.
- We will stand and together put on the armor of God, piece by piece. As we put on each piece, we will say its name and job aloud. (For example, "Lord, we are putting on your belt of truth today to protect us from lies and to help us remember your truth." Each person pretends to put on the belt, etc., until all six pieces are applied.) Everyone takes turns leading this part.
- We will close with our family motto and cheer.
- Throughout the day Dad will continue praying for the things spoken of that morning and will follow up with each person in the evening (e.g., "How did your math test go?").

Administration

- Purchase a bell.
- Secure a timer to be used to mark ten minutes.
- Get a notebook to log our meeting notes.
- Prepare the family by explaining what "Family Focus" is and what the expectations will be.
- Set the date for our first meeting.

Command

- Purchase bell, timer, and notebook—Dad
- Explain to the family and schedule our first meeting—Dad
- Have a solid understanding of the armor of God and how each piece serves us—Mom and Dad
- Be consistent about meeting daily until this becomes a family habit—All

---

Encouragement from the Homefront . . .
A Letter from Becky

Brave Soldier,

I know that equipping your family isn't an easy task. Most of us weren't equipped by anyone when we were young, so we're hard pressed to know how to teach our families. I sincerely thank you for every effort you're making to learn how to do it and to follow through.

One of the best things Jeff did for us was to speak truth and positive encouragement to us. He helped us stay focused on God. This was a skill he developed over the years because he was willing to learn. He put down his pride, didn't worry about how awkward it might seem, and just started saying good things.

There was nothing sweeter to me than to listen to Jeff and Jon Alex during their time at the swing. I would typically be in the kitchen doing the dishes and would hear Jeff speaking life over Jon Alex, telling him how much he loved him and how proud he was of him. Every night before bed, the last thing Jon Alex heard from his dad was "I love you" and "Goodnight, Superman." Jon Alex understood that he was loved and knew he was safe.

Of course, the only way to really equip our families is to lean into God's wisdom for our own lives. I've got to be honest with you that this hasn't been easy for me lately. I'm brokenhearted without Jeff and finding it hard to press into God right now. Maybe you struggle too. Let's commit to being open and asking God to help us.

Soldier, I know there are so many principles being given to you. Don't get overwhelmed. This process takes time. Just pick one thing to focus on and move forward in it. You can do hard things! Onward!

Blessings from the Homefront,
Becky

MISSION CRITICAL

- ☐ Humble yourself and submit to God.
- ☐ Determine to equip your family for the battle you're in—good versus evil.
- ☐ Train them in the principles we have discussed, and prepare them for life as a person who knows their source, their self, and their role as a servant/image bearer.

CHAPTER 8

Emotional Land Mines

Land mines were first used on a wide scale in World War II. Since then, they have been employed in many conflicts, including Vietnam, Korea, and the first Gulf War. A key characteristic of a land mine is that it is intentionally designed to maim rather than kill a soldier. The strategy behind this kind of assault is that it takes more resources and effort to care for a wounded soldier than a dead one. A land mine is designed specifically to weaken, drain, erode, and undermine the strength and morale of your opponent.

On the battlefield, a soldier is faced with life-threatening scenarios at every turn. Some are obvious; others are hidden. So it is in our struggle as dads. Over the years, I have sat with many fathers who, like me, find themselves caught up in the battle to protect and defend their special-needs families. In the battle, we encounter emotional land mines planted strategically and intentionally by the Enemy to sabotage our success, undermine our courage, and crush our spirits. They are intended not to kill us but rather to render us ineffective, to wear us down. Over the years, I have experienced more emotional land mines than I wish to recall. They've been one of the most challenging parts of my job as a special-needs soldier. I hope that by exposing the ones most common to all of us, I can help you watch your step. There are seven major land mines we will expose.

MIND YOUR STEP: SEVEN COMMON LAND MINES

In my years as a mentor, I have come to identify seven strategic emotional land mines that threaten almost all of us. We'll review each one of them so that you can be on guard as you plot your course through the challenges of this life. Be aware that you can stumble on an emotional land mine at any time, and just because you've experienced one doesn't mean you're immune to the same thing happening in the future. Your best defense is to be alert and on guard. Ask God daily to protect you and your family from these destructive traps.

The Blame Game

From the earliest moments of this journey, you must be on the lookout for the emotional land mine of blame. It's part of our human nature to want to lay blame. Blaming others serves as a defense mechanism to help us preserve our self-esteem. We ask, Why did this happen to us? Whose fault is it? Am I being punished? Am I to blame for this? These are some of the questions that torment many parents whose children have special needs.

My wife and I wrestled with these questions for many months . . . until one Scripture changed everything for us: "As [Jesus] passed by, he saw a man blind from birth. And his disciples asked him, 'Rabbi, who sinned, this man or his parents, that he was born blind?' Jesus answered, 'It was not that this man sinned, or his parents, but that the works of God might be displayed in him'" (John 9:1–3 ESV). The words leaped off the page—especially the last few: "but that the works of God might be displayed in him."

What the disciples were asking Jesus was essentially the same question I had been grappling with. My guess is that you have asked it too. The disciples encountered a man born with a disability: blindness. Someone must have been to blame, right? This had to have been someone's fault. They too were searching for an explanation—for someone to pin the blame on. Yet Jesus declared that this man had been born blind so that the works of God could be displayed in his life. Some translations even say "the power of God" or the "glory of God." Is it possible that my son's special needs might be part of God's plan to display his power?

Is it possible that God wants to use your child's life to bring glory and honor to his name? Does God really have a plan and a purpose for our special children's lives? Could it be his intention to take our suffering and redeem it to demonstrate his glory? Might God allow something so difficult to happen because what he plans to accomplish through it is far greater and more significant for his ultimate purpose?

In Psalm 139 God declares that our children are fearfully and wonderfully made just the way they are. Not only that, but he knows their life stories. He has a plan for *all of* their lives. When I first grasped this concept, I was stunned. I grabbed a legal pad and jotted down, "Wonderfully made . . . created for a plan and a purpose . . . destined to glorify God."

I decided in that moment that those words would be what I would use to describe our son. The world would say he's autistic or challenged, but I chose instead to say of him, "He is wonderfully made, created for a plan and a purpose, and destined to glorify God."

God created my son *in his own image*. God decreed that he would be wonderfully made.

God had declared it, and I chose to believe it. Yes, Jon Alex is still afflicted with cerebral palsy, but God created my son *in his own image*. God decreed that he would be wonderfully made, and he determined a plan for all the days of his life. It was written down long before he was born.

The fact that our children have special needs or disabilities doesn't catch God by surprise or point to a glitch in the system. To search for someone to blame implies that there has been a mistake. Scripture clearly states that the presence of such disability, however, is no mistake. The sooner we recognize and accept this, the sooner we can quit playing the blame game. Blame is an emotional land mine that can destroy our forward progress, keeping us stuck in a futile game of whodunit. Stay alert and avoid this trap.

Death of Dreams

We all had hopes and dreams for what fatherhood would look like. We all had expectations for the life we'd live with our children. As parents of children with special needs, we must often watch those dreams slip away. It's never easy to let go, but it's essential to our survival to improvise and adapt. The military directive is "improvise, adapt, and overcome." This mental flexibility is essential to the success of your mission. One of the easiest land mines to trip over is the temptation to hold on to our initial expectations of who and what our child will be.

I have counseled so many dads who find it difficult to lay these dreams aside. I have met men who can't lay down their plans for their own lives, even when parenting a child with special needs requires it of them. I have a friend whose life is so wrapped up in football that it has affected his relationships with both his typical son and his son with special needs. The typical son doesn't share his father's interest in football, and the son with special needs lacks the capacity to care about football at all. This dad finds it impossible to relate to, engage, or even connect with his kids because his plans and dreams for their lives were so wrapped around his obsession with a sport.

Your dreams may have to change. Your standards may have to be altered. Some of your dreams may even have to die. But whose dreams were they, anyway? God has plans and dreams for our children too. We must vigorously pursue his plans with everything in us, even if that means sacrificing our own dreams. Every child has a destiny. Every child has a path designed by God for his or her life. That means that we must surrender our own expectations so that their lives (and ours) can be all about his glory. Keep a close eye on your expectations. They can lead you straight to a land mine that, if triggered, can knock you out of the fullness of God's best for your life.

Envy

I wish I could tell you that once you encounter the envy land mine, you'll never have to deal with it again, but that's a lie. You're going to run into it again and again throughout your journey. Every time you watch someone else's child doing something yours can't, you'll be tempted. Every time you watch another child achieve something your child will never be able to accomplish, envy may crop up. There are no winners when you play the comparison game. The only way to win is to refuse to play.

The comparison game has exploded in recent years with the advent of social media. Facebook, Instagram, Twitter—we're fast becoming a society that abuses this format for instant gratification and to elevate our own status. I tell parents all the time that they can't compare their lives to those of their friends on Facebook. You have to remember that social media feeds are nothing more than highlight reels. For the most part they don't reflect ordinary life but just the highlights.

One year we found ourselves creeping toward the dark side of depression after looking at seemingly endless photos on Facebook of other families traveling to the beach or to Disney World. We decided that, rather than mourn our own inability to do the same, we would fabricate a trip on Facebook. We photoshopped pictures to create the illusion of our son visiting the pyramids, viewing the Eiffel Tower, meeting the queen of England, walking on the Great Wall of China, and appearing at a host of other sites around the world. We had so much fun with our fake trip around the world!

It's so easy to be envious of others. It's unavoidable, frankly. But there's always a flip side. The choice is ours.

Our journey as special-needs parents is uniquely different—often much harder and more frustrating than the journey of typical families. These two modes of living are too different to even be compared. It's so easy to be envious of others. It's unavoidable, frankly. But there's always a flip side. The choice is ours.

We must remember that everything God does, he does to accomplish his purposes and to bring glory and honor to his name. Our struggles become his stage; our trials, his triumphs; our weaknesses, the revelation of his strength; and our responses, reflections of his glory.

The way we respond to the challenges of raising a child with special needs, the way we let God use our circumstances to accomplish his purposes, the way we respond to the trials we face—all are part of the way we tell our story. And the way we tell our story becomes the way we live his story. God has given each of us a unique life. We have no business envying someone else's story just because it isn't our own. We have no business trying to live vicariously through someone else's story.

Beware of envy. It is a land mine buried beneath us, but it's close to the surface and highly sensitive. The next time you let your mind wander there, be extremely cautious about where you place your feet. This mine can explode before you even realize how useless it is to want a life that would never fit you. Stay focused on the blessings you have and stick to your own story.

Missed Milestones

Each time an event or typical milestone passes and your child can't achieve or enjoy it, the temptation arises to become bitter and resentful. Our hearts break over and over at the loss of what others seem to effortlessly enjoy. Unmet milestones can cause special-needs parents to grieve repeatedly over what will never be. This silent grief is noticed and recorded by God: "You keep track of all my sorrows. You have collected all my tears in your bottle. You have recorded each one in your book" (Psalm 56:8 NLT).

It isn't wrong to grieve the loss of what you had hoped for, but the ultimate goal of this emotional land mine is to make you retreat into a cave of your own making. This cave, you believe, will protect you from further pain and spare you from suffering. But the reality is that, isolated within it, you begin to withdraw from life. This seems reasonable and completely justified at first, but the Enemy, Satan, knows that if he can get you alone and unsupported, you become an easy target.

For a while Becky and I began to withdraw from attending other children's parties or social outings. Watching other kids do things my son could never do had started to feel unbearable. Pulling back seemed a smart response at first. Why torment ourselves by participating in events that reminded us of how different our family was? It wasn't long, however, before we began to realize that we were being cut off from the pack—never a good place to be. We had to flip the script for our family.

Grieving is a very natural response to loss, and it's nothing to feel guilt or shame about; however, in order to survive, we must find things in our journey that we *can* celebrate. We must train ourselves to focus on our own highlights and accomplishments. Joy can be found in the simple successes, and contentment in the seemingly insignificant moments. It's all a matter of where we place our focus. We must be deliberate about celebrating the things that are legitimate achievements for our child, no matter how minor they may seem.

There's also comfort in knowing that God sees our pain and grief, that it doesn't go unnoticed. Psalm 56:8 reminds us that we aren't on this journey alone. God is always watching over us. He shares this life with us, and the day will come when there will be no more sorrow, crying, or pain (Revelation 21:4).

I've Been Robbed!

No carefree vacations, no spontaneous activities, no travel ball, or even dinner and a movie . . .

Do you ever feel as though you've been robbed? When we start listing the things we feel the special-needs life has deprived us of, the list can get pretty long. The land mine of loss lurks around every corner, hoping to disable us with a constant sense that we're being cheated. But we have a choice as to how we view our lives. We can wallow in despair, discouragement, and frustration over our circumstances or choose to change the way we look at life.

When I decided to choose the flip side, it changed my perspective completely. Early on, I wasted so much time feeling cheated. I used to dread the thought that my son would have to live with me all his life. Now I embrace that thought joyfully. I choose the flip side by looking at the unique opportunities I have as a special-needs dad. Because Jon Alex will live out his life with us, I'll have an opportunity to make new memories with him every day. I'll get the chance to express my love for my son every morning. What a gift!

Everything along this journey—every struggle, every challenge, and every trial—will present you with a choice. And every choice will present you with the opportunity to change your outlook. After I learned the truth that the power over every circumstance depends upon my choice of perspective, I took control over what had previously been controlling me. This one act of my will cut the trip wire to the detonator of the land mine of loss. You have the wire cutters. Start choosing the flip side.

Self-Absorption

One of the most seductive traps into which we can be lured is the temptation to make life all about ourselves. We were created to reflect the glory of God, but we often gaze into the reflective mirror and become obsessed instead with our own image. From this position we can see nothing but ourselves. Everything revolves around us. When life goes wrong, we feel sorry for ourselves. Self-pity wraps its tentacles around us and pulls us under.

The land mine of self-absorption drags you deeper and deeper into the pit of despair. The greatest danger is that you'll lose all perspective and collapse in on yourself. When a person is consumed with self, it's virtually impossible to reach him. No amount of reason can break the spell of self-infatuation. Typically, the only way out is to come to the end of yourself, which usually entails great pain and loss. Only then can you escape. I know this because I have lived it. My self-absorption was broken only by great suffering. I caution you to consider how this might apply to you. Deal with it before you have to undergo correction. A moment of self-focus is one thing, but making a career of it can be lethal.

Fear

I recognize that men aren't supposed to admit fear, but seriously, you're telling me that when your child is undergoing major surgery for the umpteenth time, or having a full-blown seizure in the back of the car, you aren't giving in to some fear? The truth is that fear lurks in the dark recesses of our lives and taunts us with thoughts of death, destruction, and ruin. It's only natural for us to fear for our children when they're ill. That fear is reasonable. The fear that lurks in a land mine, however, is a fear that mocks and belittles us, making us feel exposed and vulnerable on a daily basis.

Fear is like a virus. Once we're infected, it spreads like wildfire, consuming more and more of our thoughts. Fear wants to erode our confidence in God, to unseat our peace and incite panic. Ultimately, it wants to destroy us. I urge you to keep a close watch out for fear, either in yourself or in your family members. Attack it with truth as soon as you see it. Speak Scriptures that reverse its effect. Make it a priority to shut down fear as quickly as possible. Fear is the enemy of peace, and peace is essential if we're to hear God and relax in the security he alone offers. Allow no place for fear to reside in your home. It's a "luxury" none of us can afford.

The Vulnerable Soldier

What predisposes you to stepping on a land mine? There are some basic precautions you can take to help protect yourself from these traps. Initially, there are four general conditions that can make a soldier less vigilant and more susceptible to hitting a land mine. They're often summarized by the acronym HALT. You need to stop when you're hungry, angry, lonely, or tired because you're more vulnerable to stepping on an emotional land mine. Because you're an active-duty soldier who serves round the clock, it's important for you to be as well rested as possible. It's also essential that you eat well, resolve your own emotional conflicts, and remain in the company of your band of brothers. All these things help keep you vigilant and on guard.

The other resource we as believers have is armor. In chapter 7 we talked about putting on the full armor of God, as described in Ephesians 6. This armor isn't just for women and children. It's primarily intended, in fact, for warriors, and it's a vital part of everyday living for all of us who serve God. The armor is critical for our success, and while it's invisible to the natural eye, so are emotional land mines. They're both elements of the spiritual world. Being diligent to put on the full armor of God daily will help protect you from the damaging effects of land-mine warfare. Review each piece of armor and commit their names and purposes to memory. Ask God to cover you, piece by piece, every day. You'll be amazed at the level of protection the armor provides. Don't dismiss this instruction as trivial. It can make all the difference in your effectiveness as a godly dad.

DISARMING EMOTIONAL LAND MINES

The single most effective way to dismantle emotional land mines is to practice profound gratitude. Cultivating a spirit of thankfulness is critical to keeping your feet on the path of safety. Gratitude—genuine thankfulness for the blessings *as well as the hardships* in life—keeps us oriented toward God's goodness. God directs us to give thanks in all things because that is his will for us in Christ Jesus (1 Thessalonians 5:18). It's God's will for us to stay in a place of trust. It is only from this place that we can truly be thankful *for* every circumstance that comes our way—the situations we call good and the ones we think are not good.

The other essential tool for shutting down land mines is to choose to see things upside down. Turning your situation upside down and looking at it from a different angle allows you to envision your life in a new and more positive way. One day when I was thinking about this tool, I wrote a letter to my son's disabilities. I wanted to thank them for all that they have done for our family. Maybe reading it will give you a better sense of what I mean by seeing the "flip side":

> Dear Autism and Cerebral Palsy,
>
> I've been meaning to write to you for quite some time, but thanks to you two, I've been quite busy as you can imagine.

Over the years, I have cursed at you, yelled at you, cried at you, and tried my best to understand you. The more I have learned about you, the more I realize how little I know about you.

But there is one thing I haven't done.

I have never stopped to thank you.

That's right. I need to stop and thank you, believe it or not.

You probably don't get a lot of thank-you notes mixed in with all your hate mail; so let me try to explain.

You see, you robbed my son of his speech. Because of you, he is nonverbal and has no language.

But when you robbed my son of his speech, God decided to give him a voice and a platform.

He may not speak, but God has used his life to inspire, bless, and teach others around him. He inspired my wife and I so much we started a special-needs ministry and now we are helping encourage other families like ours on the same journey.

Hey Autism, do you remember that cave you tried to lure us and other autistic families into to live for the rest of their lives? You know, the isolated dreary cave where you want all autistic families to live in without hope?

We tried it. It just wasn't for us. So now we do search and rescue, returning to the cave over and over to show others the way out of the cave and to a better place.

Hey Cerebral Palsy, there are so many things you've robbed us from for which I need to thank you.

You've robbed me from my own pride, selfishness, and greed.
You've robbed me from my tendency to put my work above my family.
You've robbed me from living for myself instead of in service to others.
You've robbed me only caring about those who are just like me.

You've robbed me of believing there are some struggles too big for us to overcome. . . .

Since you two came into my life, I have met some amazing people because of our common association with you. Therapists, teachers, assistants, service providers—dedicated and passionate people who have crossed our path and have become part of our story—people I never might have met if it weren't for you. We've met so many special-needs families who are turning their trials into triumphs, too. . . .

God didn't take away the struggles, the pain, the challenges—he just simply used them in ways I never dreamed or you never expected.

He has used them to teach me unconditional love.
He has used them to teach me the essence of grace.
He has used them to teach me to find joy in all things.
He has used them to show me how to be content in the little things.
Really, you could say he has simply used them to draw me closer to him, help me understand him, and make me stronger through him.

You really helped me take my relationship with God to a much higher and deeper level. So thank you very much! I'm so grateful! Now I rely and lean on him more than ever.

I also want to thank you for drawing my wife and me closer together in our relationship. We have learned to cry together, laugh together, grieve together, and stand strong together because of you.

So, you see, Autism and Cerebral Palsy, I have quite a bit of gratitude for you. . . .

Regards,
Jeff Davidson[14]

A Story from the Front Line

Dale Heim lives in Tennessee with his wife, Megan, and their three children, Emily, Mackenzie, and Jack. This is a personal story from his life on the front line.

Learning to avoid emotional land mines is a skill developed over time. It is best accomplished through teamwork. My wife has been inspirational in transforming our lives to meet the needs of our son with special needs. Her guidance over the past eight years has been singular and simple: "Trust God and focus on what our son *can* do and not on what he can't do." This mantra has carried me through good times and bad.

I've encountered my share of emotional land mines over the years and have stepped directly on a few. The good news is that I have survived, and by God's grace and love, I have grown. My recommendation for other special-needs dads includes these suggestions.

First, don't lose yourself or your wife in the process of supporting your child. Many parents will throw everything they have into a crisis situation. Children with special needs certainly trigger this instinct. I call this functioning in "survival mode." Realistically, you can't sustain this level of intensity. At some point you will need to reevaluate your strategy.

Second, always be learning. Read books, attend support groups, listen to other parents, and go to therapy for yourself and/or with your spouse. The process of learning should never stop. Why? Because the more you learn, the fewer the unknowns and the better you will feel.

Finally, don't stop investing in your child with special needs. It's easy for me to invest in my typical children and harder to invest in my son with special needs. It's just that simple. My son takes more patience, time, understanding, and work. I put my son on autopilot way too often. This is a challenge I face daily. Does this make me a bad father? No. It's an area in which I need to grow.

Remember, every family has different challenges, and the foundation of our success is based on trusting God. Finally, don't lose focus on your relationship, stay connected with your spouse, and take time to get away once a year. Take a well-deserved break together, and use that time to redefine the upcoming strategy for your family.

MISSION CRITICAL

- ☐ Become familiar with emotional land mines so you can avoid them.
- ☐ Remember to HALT (avoid getting hungry, angry, lonely, or tired).
- ☐ Apply the armor of God daily, and pray for protection for yourself and your family.

CHAPTER 9

Surviving Civilian Assault

You've been chosen to be a special-needs dad, called by God to stand up for the weak, defenseless, and forgotten of this world. And I trust you're committed to doing this job with excellence. We have talked specifically about the stages of grief that must be addressed when we've been chosen for this mission. We have looked at what it means to be an absent dad and how to avoid becoming one. We've gone through boot camp together and covered in detail the four-pronged assignment: protect and defend, provide, strengthen, and equip. You have been trained to detect emotional land mines and have learned how to avoid or dismantle them. Now we're going to deal with one of the toughest military confrontations you'll ever experience: assault by civilians.

Becky and I have wept over the stories shared with us through the years of special-needs families who have been rejected, overlooked, and abused. Sometimes these accounts have been almost beyond belief. A church forbidding a child with special needs to attend services ("You are welcome, but your child is not," said the letter received by this heartbroken mother). Grandparents of children with special needs suggesting that it would have been better if they had never been born. Extended family withdrawing or cutting off contact with their disabled family member. Rude comments, glaring judgment, pity, gawking stares, hostile encounters with hateful bystanders, insults, criticisms, unsolicited "helpful suggestions" that imply parental failure, endless emails with links to "cures" that have no basis in reality, utter silence, abandonment, emotional cruelty, disrespect, and an insufferable number of "Why don't you just spank him?" comments. These are just a few of the different ways in which special-needs families are regularly mistreated.

We live in a world that has no idea how to deal with us. According to Oxford Dictionaries, the word *ignorant* means to be unknowing, or lacking knowledge or awareness, but it can also mean discourteous or rude. I'm going to apply the full definition to a good portion of the general public when it comes to how to relate to special-needs families. They simply don't know how to respond in helpful ways. They have no idea how difficult our lives are or how much we love these children who aren't typical.

Some people are well meaning, others are careless, some genuinely want to help but fall short, and still others could be described as the walking dead—numb and coldhearted. Our culture isn't producing the most sensitive and emotionally evolved people right now. So what do we do?

The first rule of military engagement when you're encountering the public is this: don't shoot civilians!

CIVILIANS ARE *NOT* THE ENEMY

As special-needs soldiers, our primary responsibility is to protect and defend our families, but we must remember that we were once civilians too. We were ignorant and judgmental—or at least I was. We didn't know how to respond when we encountered a child (or adult) with special needs. Maybe we were even cruel.

Flash forward, and here we are, members of this community—its representatives, its ambassadors. How can we change the opinions of others or stamp out the ignorance if we aren't willing to do better? How can we help people see the truth about our lives if we only return their hostile fire?

I agree that it doesn't seem fair that the oppressed population has to behave with more respect than its oppressors, but that's how every lasting revolution begins. People who know better are obliged to do better. Eventually there is a shift in perspective. Eventually change comes. Remember that your kind response to their cruelty is paving the way for a better future for the special-needs community going forward.

I want to share a story with you. A story about how God makes wrong things right.

THE BULLY

Isolated and alone, he would stand in the corner of the room, two fingers shoved in his mouth while he played with glue. Seeing an exploitable opportunity, the class bully would muscle over and dare him to eat the glue. "Eat the glue! Come on, eat it!" Wide-eyed and shaking his head no, he would eventually comply and stick a huge ball of glue in his mouth. I can still remember the bully laughing, pointing, and jeering while the class looked on in disgust.

This boy was desperate for friendship. He wanted to belong, to feel himself a part of the gang, so he would tag along, always lingering a couple of steps behind everyone else. He was perpetually the butt of the classroom joke because he was different. He had special needs. It was clear that he was both physically and intellectually challenged. He was a square peg in a round hole, that hole being a private school with a student body primarily composed of the children of educators from a nearby university. It was clear that he wasn't like them, that he didn't fit in.

The class bully would pretend to buddy up to him, but too often his intent was to make this boy with special needs the victim of a cruel joke. Oh, the humiliation he endured daily. A couple of years later, a similar situation developed with another boy. Everyone could see what was going to happen. The same bully, one of the most popular boys in the school, began to pick on the boy with special needs. Because of the bully's popularity, his classmates took their cue and joined in.

The boy with special needs just wanted to be like everyone else, but the other kids didn't leave school crying nearly every day as he did. There was no understanding, no kindness, no mercy for him. He was isolated and rejected like so many of our children with special needs.

Even though these memories are decades old, I still remember them vividly. Part of the reason they affect me so much is that I'm now the dad of a boy with special needs. I can't imagine what I would feel and how I would react if that were to happen to my son. I am also a missionary to the special-needs community, and I see the effects of bullying every day. But mostly, these memories are so vivid and scorching *because I was that bully.*

CHOSEN

I have always believed, as God reminds us through David in Psalm 139, that God wrote all the days of my life in his book before a single one of them had unfolded. That means that in the mid-1970s, when I was bullying people with special needs, God had already chosen me to be his ambassador and a missionary to the special-needs community. Even though this had been ordained for me before I was born, it seems inconceivable to me now that God would have chosen a prideful bully to become a missionary to the very community he belittled and hurt. But then I think about the apostle Paul, who was called to be an apostle of Jesus Christ even though he had been a persecutor and even a murderer of Christians prior to his conversion.

Several years ago I decided to track down the first boy in this story. I couldn't remember the other kid's name, but I remembered the name of the first boy and wanted to see him face-to-face. I wanted to apologize and ask for his forgiveness. I needed him to know that I had changed, and I wanted to atone for those childhood years. I needed him to know that who I was in grade school isn't who I am anymore.

Through internet searches and other sources, I was able to find him, still here in my hometown where we had attended school together.

I found him buried in a local cemetery, having died in 1995, when he was twenty-eight years old.

I stood at his grave and sobbed. I cried for who I had been and what I had done all those years ago. I had come to his grave seeking forgiveness, atonement, and healing. I wanted to leave my shame and sorrow there. In a still moment, the Spirit of God whisked me away in my mind to another grave. I was in front of a cave outside Jerusalem, near a skull-shaped hill called Golgotha. I knew in my heart that this image represented the grave where Jesus was buried. Here God reminded me that this was the real grave at which my forgiveness, atonement, and healing were to be found. And because of this grave, I'm no longer who I used to be.

There's hope for the civilians out there who don't respond well to the special-needs world. There's even hope for cruel sons and daughters who, in their foolishness, bring harm to the vulnerable ones of this world. We must remember the truth of the saying, "There but for the grace of God go I." In this case, it *was* me. I was the bully, and now I am the one needing help. Not only is my son a person with special needs, but so am I. I have lost one foot and am in jeopardy of losing the other. I have been in and out of the hospital countless times and have spent much of the last two years confined to a wheelchair. I have spent many days clinging to life with the help of a ventilator and have faced death repeatedly. I have been required to become a person with special needs, to learn intimately this mode of living. It is my honor to better understand the challenges of my community and my privilege to get to know my people better. Because when people know better, they do better. Myself included.

HOW TO RESPOND TO CIVILIANS

When civilians are rude, to avoid *reacting*, we must know in advance how we will *respond*. To respond is to retain control of oneself and the conversation. When we react, we often put ourselves into the ring with our opponent. When you get into the ring, they feel it, and the tension escalates. When you respond with kindness, you de-escalate the situation and may have a chance of having a positive impact. There are some basic steps you can take to ready yourself for these moments:

1. Pray for your enemies. If we're daily praying for those who persecute us, we'll prepare ourselves for the inevitable attack.

We'll have stored in our hearts what we'll need to make an effective response.

2. Remember that people are broken. We live in a big, messy world where many people feel unloved and uncared for. People's lives are adrift, and in their own fear and foolishness, they say things they shouldn't. Have mercy on them.
3. Remember how much you've been forgiven. We are charged by God to continue to forgive again and again. That doesn't mean we have to hang out and be best friends, but we must keep letting people off our hook. Let them off your hook, and put them on God's hook. He's far more capable of meting out justice and will do a better job in the long run than you ever could.
4. Have a few thoughtfully prepared statements at the ready. Get in the habit of responding to criticism with a positive statement. When someone is critical of your child, say something positive about who that child is. For example:

   Civilian: "Your son is out of control!"

   Response: "My son has autism and is actually a fascinating person, but he has difficulty controlling himself when he gets overwhelmed. His name is Aaron; let me introduce you."

   Civilian: "Why is she so noisy? It's embarrassing!"

   Response: "This is my daughter Emily; she has special needs and sometimes she makes loud noises to show her excitement. I'm not embarrassed by her at all. I'm very proud of who she is."

It's critical for you to set the tone. People will follow your lead about your child. If you believe your child is delightful and has much to offer the world, so will they. If you publicly show your child love and respect, other people will fall in line. It's up to you, not them, to say who your child is! If they verbalize something negative, return with a positive. Always invite people to be introduced to your son or daughter. They will typically either back down or move on.

Sad as it may be, some people are so uninformed that they don't see people with special needs as "real people." They speak about them as though they weren't present or treat them like a pet. It's very important to speak directly to your child, not about them in their presence. It's important to show people how to talk to them. Don't use "baby talk" with a child who is of age. This gives the impression that they are less than they are. Don't talk down to them in any way. Watch what you say, guys! Show people how to behave toward your child. You are in charge of the atmosphere.

If someone treats your child in a way you don't feel is proper, politely speak to them. Because Jon Alex is a nonverbal twenty-year-old who still plays with toddler toys, we find that people will talk down to him as though he were a little child. I suspect there are many people who wonder if this even matters. I firmly believe that it does matter because it's an issue of respect. We would prefer that people speak directly to Jon Alex in a way that reflects his age. This shows him respect and honor. So how do you correct others without offending them?

God can get into the secret places in people's hearts and reach them in ways we never could.

First, you must lead by example. Show people how you want them to treat your child. If they aren't catching the clues, gently remind them of the facts. I would say something like, "You know, Nancy, Jon Alex is twenty years old, and we want to respect that, so could you please talk to him like an adult? I know it may seem like a little thing, but it would mean a lot to us." Hopefully she'll take the correction in stride, but if not, give it some time and then try to approach the subject once again. If that doesn't work, you may have to accept that Nancy is, for some reason, choosing not to change. There could be a million explanations, but something is holding her back. At this point you can only release it to God.

I can't begin to tell you how many times I have come to the place where the only thing I could do was release a situation into the hands of God. The amazing thing is that very often, when I sincerely approach God and say, "This situation is driving me nuts and I can't change it—I'm turning it over to you," something does indeed shift. God can get into the secret places in people's hearts and reach them in ways we never could. The trick is that we really have to release the situation, to lay it down. If we hold on to it, our attitude clogs what God can do. Try turning over the "impossible" situations in your life and see what becomes possible.

Ultimately, if people don't or won't change, we have to forgive them and let it go. Forgiveness isn't only for their benefit but also for your own—sometimes primarily so. Holding on to bitter feelings will only damage you, not the person toward whom you're bitter. When you forgive, you're releasing that person from your grip, turning them over to God for correction. You're saying, "I'm not going to hold this against you any longer. It's between you and God now."

We must strike a healthy balance between protecting ourselves and being open to people.

Forgiveness is critical, but it doesn't mean you have to hang out and be best friends with the person. It's important to determine who is healthy and life affirming for your family and who is not. If you have a family member who refuses to be kind toward or accepting of your child with special needs, you don't have to include them in family events. It's up to you to determine where to draw the boundary—wherever it is you feel safe and most comfortable. And yes, this is true even if it means excluding your own mother. It's the right of every person to feel safe and respected. If being with your family doesn't provide that, then draw a line at the point at which you feel safe.

One of the by-products of being mistreated by civilians is that, because the life of a special-needs family is so challenging and overwhelming, we often feel incredibly vulnerable—so vulnerable that it seems easier to retreat into our shell and keep outsiders away. We can also be hypersensitive to things people say. It won't help our cause if we're going off on everybody who looks at our child in a funny way. We must strike a healthy balance between protecting ourselves and being open to people.

We have to be willing to let people into our lives. They need to know what your reality is like. They need to know about your child, her diagnosis, and what she can and can't do. Let's try to open up and let people in. Let people help when they can. Let them learn your systems and procedures. It helps everyone to be educated and informed. If you're by nature something of a control freak, this will be particularly difficult. Often it's our wives who have the most difficult struggle with control where our kids are concerned, because they're usually the primary caregivers, but we can fall into that category too.

If your extended family has never discussed your child's diagnosis or prognosis with you, then maybe it's time to open up and provide them with details. Let them hear the truth about your life. They'll never be able to embrace your situation—or your child—if they don't know the truth. Yes, it's a calculated risk to do this. They might not respond in the way you hope—but then again, they might surprise you. Typically, it helps to tell people your story and then ask for their help in a specific way. Give them a point of action so they can have a clear path for getting involved. For instance, you could say, "Now that you know more about our situation, we were wondering if you would be willing to . . . (pick up medications for us, go to the farmers market for us, take Sadie to piano lessons when Eli is sick, etc.)."

Let's be honest: dealing with civilians can be tricky. It's my opinion that, in this case, the best defense is a good offense. That means we must be forward thinking, open, and moving toward our goal instead of defensive and reactionary. We set the tone, we move the ball, and we say what goes. We don't react to the ignorance of others. I promise you, if you love your child with unconditional love and openly show it, you'll persuade the people around you to see them differently.

What do we stand to gain if we let people in? The best-case scenario would be that we grow our community to include not only our family but also our supporters. Ultimately, we want the world to love and respect people with disabilities as much as we do. We want to make a place for all people to feel loved and accepted. That means that we have to search our hearts for any areas in which we're less than loving and accepting of others. I'll leave that right here for you to consider.

Let me share a few closing thoughts about dealing with civilians. It's important to remember that the demands of this life can leave us and our spouses depleted and worn thin. It's our job as soldiers to oversee the condition of the troops and do what we can to relieve their burdens. The HALT (hungry, angry, lonely, tired) caution is important to keep in mind because any of these four conditions can leave us vulnerable to the temptation to go off on a civilian. We need to stay well armored and well rested. As the leaders, we must set the tone for everyone else, including civilians. All of this means that we have to show up for our people. We must lead.

What about the church? Hopefully you have a spiritual community that is supportive and invested in your family. If not, begin asking God where you need to be or whether you should introduce the idea of a special-needs ministry where you are. There are resources available to help you get started. If you're not in a church, I encourage you to consider seeking out a place that has a special-needs focus. We all need the support and encouragement that a church family can provide, but I won't hesitate to tell you that if a church isn't kind and welcoming to people with disabilities, I question how devoted they really are to the teachings of Christ. It's never what people say; it's what they *do* that tells you who they really are.

A Story from the Front Line

L. J. Coates lives in Alabama with his wife, Jessica, and their two children, Nadia and Zion. This is a personal story from his life on the front line.

Our son, Zion, was born with a rare genetic disorder called infantile neuroaxonal dystrophy (INAD). At the time of his birth, he was one of only twelve children in the United States who had the disorder, and the only African American. That put us in the smallest subgroup of special-needs families possible, having a child with a disease so rare that most doctors never see a case or even know what it is. This situation can leave you feeling very alone and vulnerable.

Infantile neuroaxonal dystrophy causes muscular issues that eventually rob the patient of voluntary movement. Lack of muscle strength causes problems with feeding and breathing that result in frequent infections such as pneumonia. We were just getting out of the NICU at Children's Hospital where we had been—again—for about seven days. During this hospitalization we were feeling especially isolated and alone. My wife approached me with an idea. She wanted to take the opportunity, at our next big family dinner, to open up and talk about Zion's illness. I don't know why, but somehow talking about his condition had never really come up with the extended family. As special-needs families, we can feel isolated and alone, but we don't always think to invite the closest people in.

When Jessica first suggested the idea, I wasn't sure what to think. She reminded me of the truth that we were just "surviving." We were giving it all we had and doing a great job, but we were lonely and barely making it. Jessica decided that we needed to open up to our family, but that meant being "seen" and possibly rejected. After talking it over, we both felt that this was the right step.

The next Sunday dinner was scheduled to be at our house. It seemed like the perfect time to talk to everyone. Our family dinners are a big affair. Jessica's parents were there, along with our siblings, brothers- and sisters-in-law, and all the cousins. It was a lovely meal, and after dinner we stood up and addressed the room. Jessica said, "I want to talk about the elephant in the room." Everyone appeared puzzled and asked what she meant. She explained that she wanted to talk about Zion. People were, again, confused. "Zion is right here and he's good, so what do you mean?"

Jessica went on to ask, "How many of you know Zion's diagnosis?" To our surprise, no one did. Jessica's mom attempted to pronounce the words, but basically no one in our extended family knew. It hit us, then and there, that we hadn't let anyone in. We had just been surviving, and we hadn't included our family in our struggles. We weren't allowing people to love on us and be with us in it.

We then opened the floor for questions. We welcomed any questions they wanted to ask, even if they seemed silly. It was incredible to find out that Jessica's only brother had been avoiding us, fearing that God was somehow punishing our family. We let people talk and share, and it was a pivotal moment for our family.

We didn't have expectations for how things would go. We just wanted to give people a chance to know us, and we hoped they would receive us. We had to be willing to accept that they might not. We had to be okay with whatever might happen. Fortunately, they opened their hearts and shared their feelings and fears. It brought us closer together and changed our story for the better.

Who do you need to open up to?

MISSION CRITICAL

- ☐ Prepare yourself for hostile encounters with civilians.
- ☐ Keep yourself in an offensive position (be forward thinking and prepared) rather than taking a defensive stance (reacting and getting set off by comments).
- ☐ Consider opening up to family and friends who don't know your story. Let people in.

CHAPTER 10

Band of Brothers

I was sitting across the table from myself.

I was actually sitting across the table from Jason, a dad who was just beginning the special-needs journey. His first and only child, a daughter, had recently been given a special-needs diagnosis, and it was really messing him up.

As I listened to him share what he was feeling and how this news was affecting him, I couldn't help but think, *This guy is me in the early years.* I could anticipate his every statement. I knew the next question he was going to ask. I knew his every emotion, doubt, fear, and thought. I was hearing my own story recounted back to me.

He didn't believe his situation could come to any good. This wasn't what he had wanted for his life or the path he would have taken. He was angry, bitter, discouraged, and looking for someone to blame. He was torn between blaming himself and blaming God. And he felt alone.

He had run into a mutual acquaintance of ours whom he hadn't seen in more than twenty years. This friend had told him a little bit about me and my story and suggested that Jason reach out. So here we were, sitting across the table from each other in a fast-food restaurant. We talked for quite a while. I didn't try to answer any of the questions going through his mind. Not yet.

As we continued to meet over the course of time and got to know each other better, I began to share with him a little more about how God had chosen him and called him to this life. I told him that his child had been created for a plan and a purpose. We talked about how God was going to use his child and their story for his glory. I helped him see his daughter as his greatest gift and biggest blessing and tried to help him dig in and thrive, even though this new journey was extremely challenging and difficult.

The greatest gifts are the unexpected ones and the best plans are the ones ordained in heaven, not dreamed up on earth.

I taught him that "normal" is whatever we decide it is. I helped him see that the greatest gifts are the unexpected ones and the best plans are the ones ordained in heaven, not dreamed up on earth. All of these important pieces came over time.

In that initial meeting he needed only to realize a couple of simple truths, so I chose to focus on those. First, I assured him that he wasn't alone. I reassured him that there was a whole community of us and that we were here for each other and for him. Second, I reminded him that I was many years further down the path and could guarantee that it was going to be okay. It wouldn't be easy, but the experience would be fulfilling in its own way. With conviction I told him, "You're going to be okay," because that was what I fully believed.

In looking back at myself in those early years, that's what I wish someone had said to me. That's what I needed to hear and to hold on to when it happened to me. So that's where I started with Jason. Eventually I told him of a God who loves him so much that he orchestrated a run-in with an old acquaintance just so he wouldn't be alone on this journey. This God had purposed to put me across the table from him so that I could help him find his own purpose. This same God had used my son's disabilities—his cerebral palsy and autism—and my son's life to help me discover my own purpose in life.

I told him that I was sharing these things because it was only a matter of time before someone else he knew was going to start down the path of raising a child with special needs. That new dad was going to be overwhelmed and desperately need help. He was going to need a friend to mentor and guide him. Then it would be Jason's turn to sit beside him and listen. He would help him find his way. And he'd think to himself, just as I did, "Wow, this guy is *me*!" And so the cycle would begin again, brother helping brother.

I'm happy to report that Jason hasn't disappointed. He has grown into a beautiful example of what a special-needs dad should be. He's a soldier for his family and for our community, and I know he'll continue on this path. He recently spoke about those early days and how hard it was to trust me, how hard it was to let himself accept help and friendship. I suspect that's the case for many men. We have a hard time initiating friendships and finding ways to bond with other men.

BUILDING BETTER BONDS

The fraternal connection among men is interesting. Close male friends are a bit of an anomaly, unless you serve in the military together or share some other deeply bonding experience. It seems that it's difficult for men to make friendships a priority in our culture, and yet research shows that we crave intimacy in our friendships just as much as women do. I have some ideas about why this is so hard for us.

In our culture men are taught from the start to compete against each other. We're encouraged to outdo each other at every turn. Who can run the fastest, hit the hardest, or spit the farthest? There is steady social pressure to defeat our male peers and be the best. Competition, not cooperation, has been the focus. By the time we're adults, we have learned to scan a room and determine the strengths, weaknesses, opportunities, and threats of our peers. Men are first competitors before they're anything else. This isn't a good foundation for friendship. When men feel obligated to compete or measure up against each other, it's hard for them to drop their guard and be open and vulnerable.

By the time most men reach high school, they're beginning to disengage from close male friendships. One obvious reason is that we become more focused on getting the attention of girls, but beyond that, a lot of pressure is put on guys to avoid anything that smacks of femininity. We want the girl, but we don't want to be seen in any way as girlish. We have to be fast, smart, handsome, and strong, and we must never be too tender, vulnerable, or sensitive. This is reinforced by the flinging of insults that smack of womanhood. In a locker room you'll often hear men being called ladies, girls, or women to suggest that they're weak or unfit. Similar insults and phrases too derogatory to mention are also thrown around between men. These barbs are designed to shame us and belittle any man who isn't seen as tough or masculine.

The impact of this pressure is that men feel as though getting too close to another man, fostering rich and deep male friendships, is being too relational and therefore feminine. This is a terrible loss for men because it restricts the fullness of who God made us to be. God is a strong, mighty leader and provider, but he is also a tender, loving, creative nurturer. To dismiss the tender part of God is to forfeit so much of the goodness we need to survive. To disassociate from the softer part of masculinity is to cheat ourselves of half of who we're supposed to be.

I can tell you this from personal experience. I have gone through great physical suffering, and as the Lord has shaped me, I have become a softer, more tender man. Before my illness, and certainly in my youth, I was an athlete and a tough guy. But after being face-to-face with death and all the closer to God, I find that he has drawn out the better part of me—the part of me that's more sensitive, empathetic, and good. I am proud to be a man, but I'm not afraid to be a more balanced man who can love well. After all, what we see in Jesus is a strong, powerful man who was at the same time tender and gentle.

Another reason it's difficult for men to foster friendships is that we lack easy ways to meet other men without it feeling weird. Women can approach each other randomly and think nothing of initiating a conversation, but with men it's different. We aren't socially allowed or encouraged to randomly approach each other. We're agenda driven, not friendship driven. If we don't have an agenda, we don't have a reason to talk to each other. It is, however, helpful to have places like church or a softball league where we can more easily connect. We need those connection points.

The reality is that we need each other. Men who have good friendships live longer and feel more satisfaction about their lives. This is all the more true for special-needs dads. We desperately need other guys who can listen and who get it. Especially if you are a single dad, cultivating deep friendships with other men who can pray with you and stand in the gap when the battle is raging is critical. On this journey you must have comrades, teachers, mentors, and fellow soldiers to survive. It's imperative that we find our band of brothers and stick together as though our lives depend on it.

Listen carefully—I'm telling you something vitally important: you can't do this on your own. You can try, but you'll run out of gas. You'll become discouraged and risk hurting the family that so desperately needs you. You may also risk your own well-being. I'm fairly certain you wouldn't consider running out onto a battlefield alone. That would be crazy—and so is the thought that you can navigate this upheaval without help.

MAN TO MAN

How does one go about making guy friends anyway? Let's face it, you can't go up to a dude and say, "Hey, let's be friends" like we did in kindergarten, but does it have to be so hard? I don't think so. The premise of friendship is the idea that two people mutually agree to form a bond over common interests, ideals, goals, or desires, and they foster that bond by investing time and intention into that agreement. Sounds a bit mechanical, doesn't it? We all know there is another element to this equation. There is the need for chemistry even between friends. We need to click in some way.

So how do you know who you will click with? Putting yourself out there is risky, and no one wants to feel rejected. How do you find people with mutual interests, and how do you make the connection?

I am going to give you a few tried and tested tips to help you man up and make friends.

Number One: Get Over Yourself!

Human beings are generally self-obsessed, which means *men* are generally self-obsessed. We worry about what other people think of us. We ruminate on how we are being perceived by others. What does she think of me? Did he think what I said was stupid? Will they like me? We can't seem to help ourselves. We become convinced that our perception of what *we think* people think about us is real, when it may be completely false. Let me tell you something you need to remember: What people think of you is none of your business!

We have to break the hold these self-obsessed thoughts have over us, and there is only one way to do it. Get over yourself. Put down the "Do I measure up?" ruler. Know who you are and who you believe God wants you to be, set your heart on serving others, and get on with it. Making friends means risking being misperceived or misunderstood. If it happens, so what! Shake it off and move on. You are tough enough to handle a little turbulence in order to find your battle-running buddies. Make the choice to shut down negative self-talk in your head and the constant need to compare yourself, and take a chance on friendship.

Number Two: Be the Kind of Friend You Want to Have

If you want to have friends, you have to be one. That means it can't be all about you. Sometimes we get into a competition trying to one-up each other. I have seen this so many times. If all you care about is coming out on top, then you will never be good friend material. Show interest in other people. Here is your secret weapon: ask questions. When you get stuck in conversation or you want to draw a person in, ask them questions about themselves, their interests, their family—anything that might give you insight into who they are. Make mental notes as you go along. What do they like? Where is their passion? What do they really care about? Knowing these things will help you be a better friend.

Number Three: Find Your Gateway

You need to find a gateway to people who might share your interests. There are many gateways to friendship. It might be through a hobby club, a sports team, a church event, a class you sign up for, or a service organization. All these gateways allow you to meet people who likely share your interest in that specific activity. This is your on-ramp to meeting like-minded people.

Once you commit to an activity and start to meet people, you can begin to see who you feel drawn to. Typically, we are drawn to people who are open and authentic, who will look us in the eye, and who share a common interest. If you want people to be drawn to you, then you have to "invite" them by also being open, authentic, and connected.

Number Four: Play Side by Side

Once you have found someone you might want to hang with, think of a way you can play side by side. This could be anything from inviting them to play a video game to going fishing together. It is easier in the early days of friendship to have an activity to do together side by side that allows for conversation but where the focus can be on the activity. This takes pressure off everyone and makes the transition to deeper friendship much easier. Going to a sports event, doing a simple project together, playing music, or seeing a movie are ways to ease into a friendship and see if there is any "chemistry" without it being too awkward. If there is no connection, it's okay. No harm, no foul. Just keep trying.

Number Five: Dig Deeper

Once you have found a bro, it is important to commit to making room for the friendship. Nothing is worse than starting something and then letting it die of starvation. Find a comfortable way to stay connected. Check in from time to time, and invest in the relationship. It might be as simple as meeting for a coffee or a meal on a regular basis. Staying committed to a friendship is the only way to keep it alive and the only way to deepen it.

It is also important to remember that going deeper means being vulnerable. You have to be willing to share what you are thinking, to open up. Guys, this is where the real magic of friendship happens. When we open up and get real with people, we learn that we share so many things, including fears and frailties. This is essential as we build a band of brothers. Digging deep allows us to unburden our hearts and tell the truth about who we really are, what hurts us, and what gives us hope. Connecting at this level makes strong battle brothers.

YOUR BAND OF BROTHERS

So who will your special-needs band of brothers be? How will you find them? What is your responsibility in this?

I have some good news and some bad news. The good news is that *you* can help birth a movement. We're in the early days of a revolution of men who are willing to take a stand for the rejected and the forgotten, the neglected and the overlooked. These men see the value of the special-needs community. They want to help our people and help each other. They want to be agents of change and do more than just survive.

The bad news is that we aren't fully organized yet, and we need your help. If you can't find a group of special-needs dads in your area, you'll need to start one. This is easy to do, and the goal is simple: meet, eat, share, care. You can be an innovator and an instigator of change for other men. You can make something new happen. The group can look and feel any way you want it to. You can help us start a revolution that can change everything for special-needs families!

You can be an innovator and an instigator of change for other men. You can make something new happen.

Here's a look at one of our meetings we call Hang Time. We meet regularly at a local restaurant and do what men do. Sitting around the table over mounds of onion rings and chicken wings, we're white collar, blue collar, and no collar. Two dozen dads who couldn't be more diverse. The one thing we have in common is that we're all dads of children with special needs. Some have been on this journey for many years, while others have just embarked.

We talk about sports, politics, work, and life in general. For one night a month, we set aside the challenges, trials, and frustrations we all experience as special-needs dads. We're just regular guys meeting after work at a sports bar, embellishing our stories and sharing life together. We need this outlet. We need each other. None of us are trying to escape the realities of our situation; we're simply taking a brief break. We talk, eat, laugh, and joke. Eventually someone will ask a question and get some advice, but the power of the evening is found in the connection. When we aren't at Hang Time, we support each other. We loan our tools or lend a hand with a project and keep the connection going. Most of all, we know we're there for each other. We're brothers.

Starting a group of your own is simpler than you might think. You can use an internet meeting platform to introduce a meeting in your area. You can also drop fliers at key locations and let your special-needs providers know you're launching a group for dads. Set a time and place to meet, and stick with it until your group begins to grow. Your band of brothers, informal as it might be, will give you a sense of purpose and could make all the difference for special-needs families in your area. It doesn't have to be complicated or touchy-feely—just guys getting together around a common purpose.

On several occasions we have met for a weekend retreat. Here's a look at that experience.

Salesmen, engineers, policemen, IT professionals, truck drivers, small-business workers, contractors, and factory workers—car by car, truck by truck, we drove up the hill to the rustic lodge. Men from different backgrounds, ethnic heritages, professions, and parts of the country, gathering together for the weekend.

No one knew what to expect. We arrived a little nervous, a little anxious, and a little unsure about the next couple of days. Over the weekend, we just hung out together. Our time consisted of a steady rotation of eating ribs, chicken wings, and pancake breakfasts, interspersed with watching football and movies, taking hikes, and having spontaneous conversations around the roaring fireplace.

No one played an acoustic guitar. No one initiated a group hug. No one suggested holding hands and singing "Kumbaya." No one was forced to bare his soul or share his innermost feelings and emotions. It was just guys being guys. I watched in awe as God began to move. Men connected with each other and spontaneously shared their stories. Dads found community, relationships, and common ground. Older dads poured wisdom into younger dads. Younger dads inspired older dads. And it all happened organically, in a casual, unscripted environment through off-the-cuff conversation.

In the occasional group session, we talked a lot about stepping into the roles for which God had called us and which he had chosen for us. We talked about having the courage to be the leaders of our families and the fathers God desires us to be for our children. There was no preaching or lecturing. I just shared from my own experiences as a member of this tribe.

A raging fire on a cold night is a powerful common denominator for men. On Sunday morning, our group of dads shared Communion together. We prayed together, after which I prayed over each man by name. They, in turn, encircled me and prayed over me. I shook with emotion and furiously choked back the massive lump in my throat, listening to them.

We proudly put on our new uniform, our T-shirts that declared "I am . . . Chosen, Called, Committed." We celebrated our newly minted friendships and felt empowered to face our challenges afresh. We came from three different states, but we departed in one united state. We still had the same struggles in our special-needs lives, but we were fully prepared to face them down . . . together.

We left a little taller and with a little swagger, a little more hope, a little more encouragement, and a lot more pride. Back-to-back we stood. Suddenly I realized what had happened to us. We were no longer special-needs dads. We were no longer a group of men raising children with special needs; we were warriors, providers, and protectors. We had found each other in a common foxhole dug for dads of children with special needs, but that no longer defined us. We had become a band of brothers, and that was precisely what we needed to keep us going.

Brother, you're going to need to find your guys. Start looking and ask God to show you who and where they are. You can make this happen. Don't get discouraged. This is important for you, and it might mean the difference between life and death for one of your men.

As you start your group, keep these things in mind. Leading a group means:

- Getting to know people as people, not according to their labels.
- Learning their names and the names of their spouses and kids.
- Getting involved in their lives when necessary, as opposed to maintaining a safe, prescribed distance.
- Becoming a good listener, not just a good talker.
- Asking more questions and then looking people in the eyes and listening to their responses.
- Remembering what they shared; being a witness to their lives.
- Thinking about how you can help them succeed and caring about what happens to them.

You can do these things. It takes being vulnerable, but you're strong enough. Your band of brothers is out there, waiting for you. The military motto "Leave no man behind" is our commitment to each other as well. Gentlemen, find your band of brothers and help save a life. The life you save may just be your own.

A Story from the Front Line

Eric Nixon lives in Pennsylvania with his wife, Candy, and their three young adult children. This is a personal story from his life on the front line.

Hope wasn't a word in my vocabulary years ago. You see, I have three young adults, all of whom have a rare primary immune deficiency disorder called common variable immune deficiency (CVID for short). It rocked our world for ten years before we finally found a diagnosis. We bounced from doctor to doctor, then from specialist to specialist, with no answers. The endless searching and mounting frustration led to depression and anger. I felt as though I didn't have any hope. I felt that God was playing a cruel joke on our family. I was angry at everyone, but my wife and children felt it the most. You see, men are good at hiding their emotions from others, but we can destroy our families in the process.

I spent years with my head in the sand, and all the while my anger and frustration were escalating. One day a friend told me about a men's support group nearby for fathers of children with disabilities. It was my first glimpse of hope. I went with two friends. There were only two other men who attended, and I wondered where all the other dads were. There had to be more of us. I felt some hope finding a few other men who "got it," but after the second meeting, the leader said he was closing down the group for lack of interest. In that moment all my anger came roaring back.

My wife, seeing my frustration, asked, "Why don't you lead the group?" Was she kidding? I needed encouragement and support, but I certainly didn't want to lead a group to get it. I kept wondering where all the other dads like me were. After praying and seeking God's wisdom, however, I did decide to start my own men's support group. At first it was slow, but as more men heard about it, they started coming. Soon my hope was surging once again. Finally, I was in the company of other men who understood the hurt and anger that comes with being a special-needs dad. I had friends who got the challenges of mounting medical bills, lack of time with your spouse, and endless doctor visits.

Men claim we don't need counseling or support groups, but that is *not* true. God didn't design men to go through this journey alone. My anger was killing me and my family, so I had to find a way to help both myself and other men. You can benefit from this type of support group too. It's easy to begin.

Find a local place to meet like a coffee shop, restaurant, or home. Meet monthly because men's schedules are busy. In our case, I provide the main course (pizza, wings, sub sandwiches) and ask everyone to bring something unhealthy to share, like chips or dessert. I encourage them to bring something we normally don't eat at home with our wives. We bond over a meal together. As men get comfortable, they're more likely to share with the group about their journey. After dinner we have a short devotional time or maybe a guest speaker or sometimes just a plain old action movie. We even have our annual original black-and-white Three Stooges movie night. Yeah, my wife doesn't get it, but men love it. Iron sharpens iron, as the Bible states. You need other special-needs fathers to help encourage you to fight another day. Maybe you'll be a source of help or strength to another man. We're a band of brothers, and together we fight.

MISSION CRITICAL

- ☐ Accept your need for brothers in arms.
- ☐ Locate a group for special-needs dads or begin one in your area.
- ☐ Devote yourself to seeing your guys succeed and experience the restoration of hope!

CHAPTER 11

Marching Orders

Brother, I believe it's your destiny to become one of the Lord's best soldiers. You've been drafted to serve in what Charles Spurgeon called the "highlands of affliction." It won't be easy, but if you allow it to happen, this life as a special-needs dad will make you a better man, a man who makes an impact with his life. It's my deep personal conviction that you've been chosen for this job because God sees something in you. He sees your strength and your potential to become more than you think you are. He has, quite deliberately, placed in your care a child who has special needs. This child, while rejected by many as imperfect, is a gift to you and to the world. But you have to flip the situation on its head to be able to see it from God's perspective.

The most powerful thing you can do is believe the truth that you've been chosen and called by God to this mission. You must then commit yourself to it without reservation. Humbly ask God to make you the man you're meant to be. This requires that you abandon your claim to your own life. It means you'll likely become someone different from the man you expected to be. If you opt to keep your life and live it by your accustomed rules, you may have some modicum of success. You may do all right by the world's standards, but you'll never know who you could have been. Life on your own terms might be easier, but it will rob you of your potential impact. Do you want to make an impact? I think you do. Accept that the path you're on as a special-needs dad is your path to becoming an influencer. This path will be the making of you. Throw yourself into this assignment and watch what God does.

This journey is, by nature, a long one. It will last the length of your life or the life of your child. This reality requires that we consider the long view. It is important to begin with the end in mind. By that I mean you need to decide what kind of family experience you want to have. Where do you want your family to end up? What kind of marriage do you want to have? How do you want to feel about your life in ten years? Spend some dedicated time considering these answers. Visualize what you want to see happening. Consider the path you must take to get there.

In the day to day of things, you must take it one step at a time and meet each challenge as it comes to you. You will have different needs at different stages of the game. I want to encourage you to return to this training manual again and again as you face new challenges. Find the words you need for the season you are in. God will show up for you if you lean into your role as a father. He will actually father you, teach you things, and provide inspiration when the going gets tough. He will use your circumstances, the people around you, your God-enlightened conscience, and hopefully the words written in this manual to raise you up and lead you onward!

WHERE DO I GO FROM HERE?

Let this book help you become a man who influences his family and community. If you are unsure where to begin, then I suggest you go back through the five stages of grief and determine whether you're stuck at any point. If you are, it's at precisely that point that you need to start. Find a brother you can talk to, pray through your pain, and stay accountable until you feel you've achieved breakthrough. Denial, anger, bargaining, depression, and acceptance are the stages we must all work through to be able to fully commit to this life.

If you feel like you have moved through the grieving stage for now (remember, you may have to return again and again to a section as new issues arise), then consider the fallout absent dads have on their families and their communities. Ask yourself honestly whether you have any tendency to drift (we talked about several potential pitfalls). If you do, ask God to help you. Ask him to draw your heart closer to your family. Abandon any distraction that's keeping you from your duties. Give your whole heart to the job you've been called to do. No real soldier would sit on the battlefield and talk on his phone or watch the game. Know where your heart is regarding your family always.

Next, review the seven core values of loyalty, duty, respect, selfless service, honor, integrity, and personal courage. These values are the plumb line for our lives. Together they constitute our code.

Know the areas in which you're strong and those in which you lack commitment. Ask God to build you up where you are lacking. Refresh yourself on the weapons of warfare at your disposal. You need to be able to use these tools skillfully; they include personal conviction, mental toughness, prayer, the Word of God, the bond of marriage, and fraternity. These are your weapons for the battle, and they help empower you to do your job well. As with anything else worth achieving, practice makes a better soldier, so become skilled by putting these to use daily.

Rehearse the specifics of each area of service on which we've focused. Your mission is to protect and defend, provide, strengthen, and equip. Give yourself a grade in each area and work to improve the deficits in those areas in which you feel yourself falling short. If you really want to dig deeply, ask your spouse how she thinks you're doing and how you can improve.

Your most important mission is to embrace your child with special needs exactly the way God created him or her.

Ultimately, your most important mission is to embrace your child with special needs exactly the way God created him or her. Love them unconditionally and passionately, with all your heart. Do some soul searching to determine how you're doing with this most critical task. If you need help, God is ready and able to give you more of what you need. You must simply ask. I often ask God to give me his love for someone if I'm lacking it on my own. He's the source of love, so he's got anything you might be lacking—and he's only too happy to share.

Review the seven land mines that are common danger areas for special-needs families: blame, the death of dreams, envy, missed milestones, feeling robbed, self-absorption, and fear. Keep in mind that you need to HALT (ask yourself if you are hungry, angry, lonely, tired) and put on the full armor of God daily to help you steer clear of land mines.

Think about the challenges you face when dealing with civilians. Are you easily provoked by others' insensitivity? Are you quick-tempered? Do you help people understand your world, or do you expect them to comprehend without any direction? Guard yourself from civilian attack by being prepared for such encounters, and keep your peace. Please, for heaven's sake, don't shoot civilians; that's hardly a positive image for us as special-needs soldiers.

Finally, locate your band of brothers. They'll be your biggest asset outside your family for succeeding as a special-needs dad. Your brothers will be the ones you can talk to when you're about to lose it, the ones who'll help you stay grounded and focused. They'll cheer you on and be there to help you up when you fall. Pray for God to draw together a band of brothers who will get you through the toughest hours and celebrate your greatest victories.

When you begin to feel overwhelmed by this process, just stop. Choose one thing to focus on. Determine your best strategy and SMEAC a plan, if needed, to meet the challenge. Face the challenge before you. Do not turn away. Do not distract yourself with other things. Man up and do the hard thing. You got this!

I want to encourage you that I truly believe you have what it takes to become a man who loves his family well and is an asset to his community. You are more courageous than you think, and you have God-given instincts that will sharpen as you go deeper. It takes time and practice, but more than anything, it takes a willingness to let go of your expectations and accept what *is*. We waste time and energy fighting things that cannot be changed when we could instead direct that time and energy toward our own personal revolution.

WORDS TO LIVE BY

I want to come back now to the rules of engagement that were mentioned in the introduction. See whether you remember them.

THE RULES OF ENGAGEMENT
Your strength will be most magnified by your surrender.
Your toughness will be displayed through your tenderness.
Your significance will be measured by your selflessness.
Your success will be determined by your sacrifice.

I suspect these statements make more sense to you now than when you first read them. I'm coming back to them because I know that if you've come this far, you're committed and have already started to change. I'll bet these rules of engagement mean more to you now. I believe you have a better understanding of what your surrender, tenderness, selflessness, and sacrifice mean for your success as a special-needs soldier.

These principles are a perfect example of God's ways being so different from our ways. We're living in a time when godly character isn't highly valued—or often demonstrated. We don't have as many living examples as I wish we had. It's moving and inspiring to see a godly man living out a life that impacts others, and I can assure you that if you'll make these rules of engagement part of your life, you'll see a change in your own family and in your world. Become a man who inspires others!

If you take this training manual to heart, you'll become a person of impact. It may be that you're meant to change the special-needs world, or you may be called to effect change in some other area within your sphere of influence, but you *will* have an impact. There are some things you need to know as you go forward, things that will empower and equip you as an influencer. I urge you to focus on the following axioms so you can maximize your efforts.

START WHERE YOU ARE

Living a life of impact means starting where you are—not where you think you should be. We often disqualify ourselves in our own minds before we even begin. We talk ourselves out of our destiny and forget that we've been created in the image and likeness of God (Genesis 1:26). We wonder, "Who am I to be a person of influence?" But in reality, you were born for this! You were wonderfully fashioned, created according to a plan and a purpose, and destined to glorify God—just as your child is. If you live your life engaged with God and focused on serving others, you'll begin to see the true power your life can have.

You may think, "I'm no pastor; I'm just an ordinary guy." Well, that's perfect because all of us begin there—right where you are. Allow yourself to envision the impact you would like to have. In what ways would you change your world? Dream big and see yourself making a difference in a specific way. Remember what Viktor Frankl, the Holocaust survivor, believed about a man's influence? You must see yourself becoming more, having purpose and destiny, not only to survive but to thrive. How you see yourself is highly correlated with what you will achieve. As a man thinks, so is he (Proverbs 23:7 NKJV).

DON'T CONFUSE LOOKING SIGNIFICANT WITH BEING SIGNIFICANT

Being a person of impact isn't the same as being famous. If it's fame you seek, then this is the wrong train. But if you want to change your corner of the world for the better, then *all aboard*! What thoughts stand in the way of your visualizing yourself as a person of impact? Do you think your past disqualifies you? Do you think your job or place in life presents a hindrance? Do you wonder if you have what it takes?

Let me assure you that one of the best aspects of being a Jesus follower is that he makes all things new. Your past can become your place of relevance. Who better to help an addict, for example, than someone who knows what it's like to have been there? As for your job and station in life, I can guarantee that there are people around you right now who need an example of a godly man who loves unconditionally. Do you have what it takes? If you focus on yourself, you'll never achieve liftoff, but if you center your thoughts and intentions on giving the love and kindness of God to those around you, you'll soar. It's seldom people of fame who become lasting agents of change. It's strong, brave soldiers like you who are willing to lay down their lives for a cause.

FIND YOUR DISCONTENT

One of the best ways to locate your area of impact is to pay close attention to your holy discontent. What is it that really troubles you about the world? What do you encounter on a regular basis that causes you to protest, "That isn't right!"? What bugs you, frustrates you, or keeps you up at night?

If you long for a sense of mission and purpose, spend some time feeding your discontent. Spend time thinking about what disturbs your sense of justice. What is it that troubles you about this life? Listen carefully and fuel that fire. Allow your emotions to become fully alive and engaged, and then carry that fire with you to the issue that needs to change. Let yourself get passionate about something that truly matters to you. Don't dumb down your feelings, your righteous anger, or your discontentment. These are fuel for the fire that creates change.

There are countless stories of people who have let their own pain motivate them to initiate change. Bill Wilson and Dr. Bob Smith were hopeless alcoholics for years. They came together to found Alcoholics Anonymous and have helped millions of people as a result. Evelyn Stone's mild forgetfulness turned into serious mental deterioration right before her husband's eyes. As a result, Jerome Stone, a Chicago businessman, felt the need to establish the Alzheimer's Association to help other husbands and family members cope with the tragic loss this disease brings. Your pain or struggle may be your motivator. Your tragedy may become someone else's salvation.

DON'T BE AFRAID TO LOSE YOURSELF

We have been called to be the salt of the world (Matthew 5:13). Have you ever eaten unseasoned meat? It's unbelievable what a little salt can do for a meal, and yet salt is at its best when it gets lost in the flavor of the meal. In the same way, we're called to lose ourselves in God's greater plan and play our part in enhancing his glory.

God is painting on a canvas as large as the universe, while you and I are living in a 5x7 photo. We try so hard to figure out the big picture, but we have access only to the area within this little frame. God's story began long before us and will continue after we are gone. We must find our place in the story and live our destiny so that his will may be accomplished. Yes, your life is directly connected to God's will being fulfilled—or not. Don't play small, soldier. Don't play small.

STRENGTHS VERSUS WEAKNESSES

You need to know that our big God will use your strengths *and your weaknesses* for his purposes. You don't have to fear that you aren't enough. Oftentimes it's our weaknesses that set us up for future success. Our failures teach us humility, and that humility can open the door to greater opportunity. If God knows he can trust your heart because you're humble, he can use you for more.

Humility is often misunderstood in American culture. Humility isn't the "Aw shucks!" resignation we often see even among Christians. It's a deep and certain knowing that everything good that comes from you is sourced in God. You need to have it settled in your heart that anything good you accomplish is God-born. You have no goodness of your own—nor do I. Your strength and your weakness both belong to God. Give him all of you and let him show you what he can do.

I once heard a story about a young man who had Down syndrome. He was attending a conference where he heard a speaker share about the power of influence. The point was made that every interaction with a person is an opportunity to create a memory. That young man took those words to heart. A bagger at a grocery store, he hatched a plan. Every day after work he would come home and choose a saying for the day. He would handwrite it out six times on a page and make fifty copies. Slowly and deliberately he would cut out all three hundred messages and take them to work the next day. As people were checking out, he would slip one in their shopping bag. As they were leaving, he would look them in the eye and tell them he had put a gift in their bag and that he hoped it would help them have a good day. In no time, word got around and people would stand in his line, despite how long it grew, just to get their daily dose of encouragement.

Your strength and your weakness both belong to God. Give him all of you and let him show you what he can do.

This young man used what he had. He yielded his strength and his weakness to God. He didn't hide behind his disability or make excuses for himself. In fact, the purity of his heart made his gesture even more powerful and meaningful to his customers.

What are your opportunities? The goal of simply encouraging others is far more powerful than you can imagine. People are hurting. All around you people ache with pain, disappointment, and loss. Your one act of kindness can shift some of the burden, ease their pain, and infuse them with a little hope. Do you know the value of hope? You know it's priceless once you've lost it. Decide what your path of impact should be and get in the game! Don't sit on the sideline any longer.

GOD IS IN IT ALL

There's nothing in your life that God didn't either allow or orchestrate. I'm going to say that again: there is nothing in your life that God didn't either allow or orchestrate. Our choices matter, and they affect the course of our lives, but God is sovereign, and he rules over all. He can work all things together for your good, even when they seem utterly hopeless. He can take any challenge you face, any difficulty, and make you better through it. To become a better person isn't always our top priority, but it is his when it comes to his purpose and plan for us. His endgame is to help us become more like Christ. God has a plan to bring glory out of your darkest hour. He has a mission for you, and he'll help you fulfill it, but the outcome belongs to him. Our joy is the unimaginable privilege of getting to partner with the Creator of the universe. We get to work with God to see his agenda accomplished. What an incredible honor!

GOD BELIEVES IN YOU!

The fact that you have a mission from God means that he believes you're up to the challenge. The Bible is abundantly clear that we were created for good works, which God long ago prepared for us to do: "For we are God's masterpiece. He has created us anew in Christ Jesus, so we can do the good things he planned for us long ago" (Ephesians 2:10 NLT).

If he first designed and then created you, if he planned your days on the earth and gave you good works to do, then why would he set you up to fail? Would you set your child up to fail? Do you dismiss her when she makes mistakes? Of course not! Then why would your heavenly Father do that to you? The only way to fail is to refuse to try. Forget the mistakes and failures you'll undoubtedly make. Forget the difficulty you will no doubt face. Give yourself completely to your mission, and enjoy the satisfaction of the Lord's good pleasure in you. Be a person whose life has eternal impact. Play the game to the very end, with all your heart; there's no possibility of failure if you give your all.

Your mission is proof that God believes in you, and so do I. Go out, soldier, and change the world! You have what it takes.

Winston Churchill is widely considered one of the twentieth century's most significant figures. He is remembered and respected for his wartime leadership and his fight for the survival of democracy. His style was brash and often offensive, but he understood that determination and commitment to the cause were essential. It was from him that we have quotes like, "For defeat there is only one answer . . . victory" and "It's not enough to float. We have to swim."

Gentlemen, I have given my whole adult life to seeing the special-needs community begin to get the love and attention it needs and deserves. The path before us is no doubt full of obstacles and challenges, but I believe this mission to be of utmost importance. I believe that it will fall to us to educate others about who we are and how valuable our children are to this world. I believe we will have to empower ourselves to act on behalf of our own community. As Gandhi said, we will have to be the change we want to see.

Remember when I was sitting across the table from Jason and I told him it was no accident that he had bumped into a friend who sent him my way? Well, I believe it is no accident that you are reading this book. I have prayed for you. I have cried out to God for you, and I believe you are part of the answer to my prayers. Join me in this fight for your children and for our community.

★ ★ ★

In these final moments together, I want to challenge you to show up for the life you have been given. Become a man who others will follow, a man who is respected and appreciated because he is committed to the cause. Don't die without living to the fullness of your potential. Don't quit before you have even started. Embrace the fact that you are a common man with an extraordinary call. Know that you can be a part of making history in the kingdom of God.

I leave you with the same encouragement that King David spoke to his son Solomon as David handed him the plans for the construction of the temple. David received detailed plans for the temple from the heart of God and he put immense time and energy into its preparation, but he was not allowed to build it. Solomon was the one the Lord used to build his temple and it was a magnificent temple indeed.

Many years ago, God gave me a dream. He called me to be a soldier and to build an army of brothers who are devoted to their families and to protecting and defending the special-needs community. Like David, I may not be allowed to finish this dream, but I am giving you the plans and I am calling you my "son." Brave soldier, I need you to step up.

> **David also said to Solomon his son, "Be strong and courageous, and do the work. Do not be afraid or discouraged, for the LORD God, my God, is with you. He will not fail you or forsake you until all the work for the service of the temple of the LORD is finished." (1 Chronicles 28:20)**

May the Lord empower you to fulfill your destiny and live the life you were born for.

Remember that he is with you and he will not fail you or forsake you!

I believe in you.

Chosen, Called, Committed,
Jeff

AFTERWORD

A Letter from Becky

Brave Soldier,

Congratulations! You have successfully completed basic training and are poised to become a man of impact in this world. Jeff would be so proud and honored that you've come this far.

I want you to know how desperately you're needed in this fight. As I adjust to the reality of my own life without Jeff, I'm keenly aware of how difficult this special-needs life is without a partner. I plead with you on behalf of your wife and children to bring your best to your family. We need you more than we could ever express.

Thank you for all the ways you love and serve your family. Your actions are life-giving to our whole community. You inspire other men when you live well. You infuse us with dignity and courage when you show up strong for us.

I'm going to ask you one thing: Would you commit to helping Jeff's dream become a reality? Would you build the strength of the special-needs community by encouraging other men like yourself? Help new dads, encourage them, call them up, and equip them as you're able. Take a band of brothers and lead them to victory. Show other special-needs families what it looks like to thrive. Help us create a movement of men who don't hold back, who run to the aid of their own. The special-needs community needs what you have to offer. You aren't here by accident. You have purpose, and God has a plan.

Blessings from the Homefront,
Becky

APPENDIX

A Band of Brothers Study Guide

Soldier, as you know, it's one thing to have a rifle, but without bullets it's of little use. So it is with this book. It's one thing to read but quite another to internalize the principles and follow through with action. I encourage you to take this book to your band of brothers and talk about its impact on your life. Sit down together and hash out the guts of what we've talked about. Exercise your mind and will. Build up your strength together. If you walk through this study as brothers, you will tighten the bond among you and the impact will be greater. Together we overcome . . . no man left behind.

We know that your time is valuable, so this study is designed to be completed in just four sessions. You will need to have read the material for the chapters to be discussed before you meet. The group study could be easily accomplished in monthly meetings. The breakdown is as follows.

Session 1—Foreword, Preface, Introduction, and Chapters 1–3
Session 2—Chapters 4–6
Session 3—Chapters 7–9
Session 4—Chapters 10–11, Afterword

The questions are divided into chapters so that if you're able to meet more frequently, you can cover one chapter at a time.

Onward!

SESSION 1

Chapter 1

In the beginning of the book, Jeff talks about being in "the belly of the beast" after learning that Jon Alex would face life with great challenges.

1. Can you relate to that description? What does "the belly of the beast" mean to you?

2. Explain how you felt upon receiving your child's diagnosis.

3. Read Psalm 13:1–3. What does this passage mean to you?

Our culture tells men that they can't and shouldn't feel emotions such as depression, loss of faith, lack of focus, humiliation, guilt, rage, the need to "fix it," or anger. I'm here to tell you that I felt many of these emotions, and you probably do too.

4. Which emotion from this list do you most identify with and why?

In her book *On Death and Dying*, Elisabeth Kübler-Ross discusses the five stages of grief: denial, anger, bargaining, depression, and acceptance.

5. Have you gone through any or all of these stages regarding your child's special-needs diagnosis and condition?

Chapter 2

One of the greatest challenges a man will ever face is to be confronted with a situation that leaves him feeling powerless and unable to "fix it."

1. Explain what happens when you feel defeated before you even start.

2. What's your kryptonite—something you know you can't fix about your child that makes you feel powerless?

Viktor Frankl wrote in his book *Man's Search for Meaning* that we have a choice as to how we'll live and that it's important to choose to live with purpose.

3. How are you responding to this season of your life?

4. What do you see as your purpose?

As men, we must guard ourselves from the temptation to drift or walk away from our families. It's all too easy to become an absent dad.

5. In chapter 2 there are twenty-five warning signs of becoming an absent dad. Which are you currently struggling with?

6. What three things can you do right now to prevent yourself from becoming an absent dad?

Chapter 3

In basic training there are three distinct phases: red, white, and blue. In chapter 3, we discussed the red and white phases.

In the red phase there are seven core values (loyalty, duty, respect, selfless service, honor, integrity, and personal courage).

1. Which two values are the easiest for you, and which two are the most difficult? Why?

2. It has been said that some of the toughest battles we'll ever fight are in our own minds. Do you find this to be true? If so, how?

3. Do you have a close friend or mentor who understands your family's unique situation? If so, explain how this helps.

Read Psalm 56:3–4.

4. What does this passage mean to you?

SESSION 2

Chapter 4

Consider the impact your father had on you.

1. How did your dad do in the areas of protecting and defending, providing, strengthening, and equipping your family while you were growing up?

2. In what ways do protecting and defending, providing, strengthening, and equipping look different when your child has special needs?

3. Do your own risk assessment of how you're currently doing in each area. What areas do you need to work on?

This chapter talks about how our special-needs families are already highly stressed and how we need to be the "gatekeepers."

4. How do you keep unnecessary chaos and drama away from your family?

Chapter 5

It's easy for us to feel as though we're in charge of our own destiny and that we don't really need to lean on God.

1. What happens when you leave God out of your family and life?

In this chapter, Jeff talks about the example you are to your children and how this is arguably the most important thing you "provide" them.

2. In what ways are you succeeding as an example? Where do you need to improve?

Your example is one thing about you that your family will remember long after you're gone.

3. What will your spouse and children remember most about you?

The book lists ways we provide for our family that do not involve money, such as being consistent, providing a place to vent, providing opportunity to fail, giving hope and inspiration, being fun, teaching what it means to be a good man, and providing spiritual guidance.

4. Which of these do you do well? Where can you improve?

Chapter 6

Of all the behaviors and actions that can fortify your family, speaking life and encouragement to them is one of the most vital.

1. Do you find that speaking encouragement comes naturally to you, or is it a challenge?

Read Psalm 23. David alludes to self-care being essential, intentional, and focused.

2. What are you doing to make yourself a better spouse and dad?

Oftentimes mothers are the primary caregivers, and for the most part women have more difficulty allowing themselves time for self-care.

3. What are you doing to encourage and ensure that your spouse has equal self-care time and opportunity?

As dads, one of the best ways to protect our families is through prayer.

4. What specifically are you praying for regarding your spouse and children?

SESSION 3

Chapter 7

Chapter 7 is about equipping your children to know who their source is, who they are, and why they are here. I think this is one of the most challenging sections of the book because it takes focus and a very intentional strategy to succeed at it. You also have to know the answers to these questions for yourself.

1. Have you settled the following questions in your own mind and heart: Who is your source? Who are you? Why are you here?

2. Each time you instruct your children about the Lord, why is it important to ask God to translate what you're saying so that it touches their hearts and minds?

3. If your child is nonverbal, do you believe their spirit can comprehend more than their minds can? What do you base this belief on?

4. How can you teach your children that God is their one true source of wisdom, protection, and provision?

It's important to teach our children how to combat fear, which can completely derail us.

5. How do you address fear in your home and in your own life?

Chapter 8

The world is full of emotional land mines planted strategically and intentionally by the Enemy to sabotage our lives and families. There are seven common emotional land mines that were covered in the book: blame, death of dreams, envy, missed milestones, feeling robbed, self-absorption, and fear.

1. Tell about a time you stepped on one of these land mines in your own life.

It has been said that the best way to disarm emotional land mines is by developing a heart of gratitude.

2. What does that look like in your life? Are you prone to being grateful, or is it hard for you as it was for Jeff in the early years?

3. What does the acronym HALT mean? When have you been tripped up by some of these conditions in your life?

4. How could recognizing the HALT conditions early help us as husbands and dads?

Ephesians 6:10–17 commands us to put on the full armor of God.

5. Were you aware that this is a command and that it is meant to protect and defend you? How can you personally create a routine that includes this practice?

Chapter 9

Sometimes well-meaning people can be careless and cruel to us as parents because they don't understand our children. Sometimes the civilian assault even comes from those closest to us, including parents, grandparents, neighbors, extended family, and—yes—even the church.

1. How do you respond to cruel or thoughtless comments?

2. Tell about a time when you felt overwhelmed and frustrated with someone who didn't understand your unique family.

The first rule of military engagement when encountering the public is "Don't shoot civilians." It can be hard not to lash out at people who are mean-spirited and cruel to our families.

3. When has this happened to you, and how did you respond?

We as representatives of the special-needs community need to be like missionaries to help educate people, but too often the stresses of life get the better of us.

4. How can you practically help educate others about your specific family?

Jeff talks about four ways to respond to civilians:

Pray for your enemies.
Remember that people are broken.
Remember how much you've been forgiven.
Have a few thoughtfully prepared statements at the ready.

5. What is your typical response to rude civilians?

Ultimately, if people won't change, we must forgive them and let it go.

6. Are you holding on to some resentment or anger against someone who has hurt your family?

SESSION 4

Chapter 10

God has called us as special-needs dads to live a different kind of life and to function as salt and light to the world.

1. Do you feel up to the challenge, or do you feel as though this just isn't fair?

2. Do you think you would benefit from belonging to a band of brothers? What benefits might come from it?

3. What do you think are the dangers of traveling this journey alone?

Chapter 11

You were chosen and called by God to this mission as a special-needs dad.

1. Do you believe the above statement? Why or why not?

THE RULES OF ENGAGEMENT

Your strength will be most magnified by your surrender.
Your toughness will be displayed through your tenderness.
Your significance will be measured by your selflessness.
Your success will be determined by your sacrifice.

2. How has your understanding of "The Rules of Engagement" changed after reading this book?

3. As special-needs dads, we're often reluctant or afraid to lose ourselves within something bigger. Why do you suppose this prospect feels so threatening?

4. Thinking back through what you read in this book, assess and write out what you see as your top three strengths and weaknesses.

5. Can you identify anyone who could help you improve upon your weaknesses?

6. How can you specifically commit to strengthening dads within the special-needs community and helping to encourage other men like yourself?

IMPROVISE. ADAPT. OVERCOME.

THRIVE.

FIND USEFUL TOOLS AND RESOURCES @ WWW.COMMONMANEXTRAORDINARYCALL.COM

- Watch videos from Jeff and a personal message from Becky
- View additional media, including messages from other dads who have children with special needs
- Download printable resources for yourself and your family
- Find out more about Rising Above and other ministries that serve the special-needs community
- Link to blog posts from Jeff and other bloggers in the special-needs community
- Get encouragement and inspiration designed for your journey

NOTES

1. I compiled this definition after reading numerous articles on the strategy of shock and awe. Almost all information on this topic originates from Harlan K. Ullman and James P. Wade, *Shock and Awe: Achieving Rapid Dominance* (Washington, DC: NDU Press, 1996), https://www.gutenberg.org/files/7259/7259-h/7259-h.htm.
2. "Depression," American Psychological Association, accessed October 19, 2018, http://www.apa.org/topics/depression/.
3. Victor Frankl, *Man's Search for Meaning* (New York: Pocket Books, 1963), 104.
4. G. K. Chesterton, "Christmas and Disarmament," *Illustrated London News*, January 14, 1911.
5. Francis B. Carpenter, *The Inner Life of Abraham Lincoln: Six Months at the White House* (Lincoln, NE: University of Nebraska Press, 1995), 258–259.
6. Abraham Lincoln, "Letter to Quintin Campbell," in *The Collected Works of Abraham Lincoln*, ed. Roy P. Basler, vol. 5, *1861–1862* (New Brunswick, NJ: Rutgers University Press), 288.
7. Jill Bolte Taylor, *My Stroke of Insight: A Brain Scientist's Personal Journey* (New York: Penguin, 2008).
8. Charles Grandison Finney, "Jesus Christ Doing Good," *Oberlin Evangelist* 13, no. 21 (October 8, 1851), https://www.gospeltruth.net/1851OE/511008_doing_good.htm.
9. George Müller, *The Autobiography of George Müller* (Springdale, PA: Whitaker House, 1984), 16.

10. George Müller, *Autobiography of George Müller: A Million and a Half in Answer to Prayer* (Vestavia Hills, AL: Solid Ground Christian Books, 2004), 693.
11. Roger Steer, *George Müller: Delighted in God* (Tain, Ross-shire, Scotland: Christian Focus, 1997), 131.
12. Adapted from the list found in George Müller, *Answers to Prayer from George Müller's Narratives*, compiled by A. E. C. Brooks (Chicago: Moody Press, 1897), ebook.
13. Jeff Davidson, *No More Peanut Butter Sandwiches* (Colorado Springs: Crosslink, 2014), 116.
14. Davidson, *No More Peanut Butter Sandwiches*, 223–226.

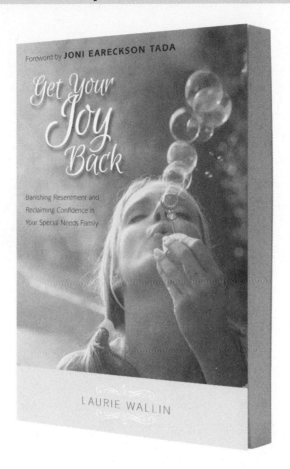